C000056208

AMAZE your CUSTOMERS!

creative tips on winning & keeping your customers

daniel zanetti

KOGAN
PAGE

London and Philadelphia

Publisher's note
Every possible effort has been made to ensure that the information contained in this book is accurate at the time of going to press, and the publishers and authors cannot accept responsibility for any errors or omissions, however caused. No responsibility for loss or damage occasioned to any person acting, or refraining from action, as a result of the material in this publication can be accepted by the editor, the publisher or any of the authors.

First published in Germany in 2003 by Redline Wirtschaft as *Kundenverblüffung: Kreative Tipps, wie Sie Ihre Kunden nachhaltig an sich binden*

First published in Great Britain and the United States in 2006 by Kogan Page Limited
Reprinted 2006

120 Pentonville Road
London N1 9JN
United Kingdom
www.kogan-page.co.uk

525 South 4th Street, #241
Philadelphia PA 19147
USA

© Redline Wirtschaft 2003, 2006

The right of Daniel Zanetti to be identified as the author of this work has been asserted by him in accordance with the Copyright, Designs and Patents Act 1988.

ISBN 0 7494 4557 2

British Library Cataloguing-in-Publication Data

A CIP record for this book is available from the British Library.

Library of Congress Cataloging-in-Publication Data

Zanetti, Daniel
 [Kundenverblüffung. English]
 Amaze your customers! : creative tips on winning and keeping your customers / Daniel Zanetti.
  p. cm.
 Includes index.
 ISBN 0-7494-4557-2
 1. Consumer satisfaction. 2. Customer services. 3. Competition. I. Title.
HF5415.335.Z36 2006
658.8'343—dc22
                               2005030518

Typeset by Jean Cussons Typesetting, Diss, Norfolk
Printed and bound in Great Britain by Creative Print and Design (Wales), Ebbw Vale

Contents

Acknowledgements

I would like to thank everyone who has amazed me and made my life as a customer sweeter over the last 38 years. On my frequent trips, on business and for pleasure, I have again and again met people who, in their everyday lives, set an example of what this book is all about, namely providing outstanding service. And if now and then the service is not so good, I have found a way to voice my frustration as a customer through the mouth of Joe Friedmann.

Thank you also to:

My son **Noah**, the best thing I ever did. He teaches me so much, and he has the whole of his amazing life in front of him. I will be there for you, always!

My partner **Beatrice**, whom I honour above all others and who is the focus of my life. Your love gives me so much.

Jörg Neumann, my friend, my source of inspiration and ever-dependable business partner. I hope we work on many more exciting projects together!

Heike Reutlinger, who has contributed so much to the success of this book with her enthusiasm and her identification with its message. I couldn't do without her. Thank you, Heike!

Harry Gisler, who has been my role model in matters of customer-orientation for many years.

My postman, who not only delivers my mail, but also spreads a little good cheer every morning.

The NeumannZanetti & Partner Dream Team, who work very hard with us to ensure that we remain an outstanding company.

Daniela Amrein, a pillar of support. What would I do without you? You manage to do a thousand different things at once and still you never forget to smile.

Alexandra Furrer, who has been at my side for many years. With your amazing flexibility and your contacts, you always manage to provide support in the right place and at the right time.

Bettina Spichiger, our fantastic trainer. I can always rely 100 per cent on you. I am in awe of the way you manage to strike the perfect balance between work and fun.

Aurelia Marty, the perfect office manager we always dreamed of. It is your firm hand that holds the reins inside the company. You are a blessing for our company in every way.

Ralph Hubacher, our 'master tailor'. You manage to come up with a tailor-made solution for every new client and, with your friendly manner, your consistency and courage, you ensure that our company stays on the right track.

Lucia Elmiger, our woman for every eventuality! Thank you for rounding off our team so perfectly for so many years. You never cease to amaze us all with your professionalism and inspiration.

Ina Stockhausen, our woman in Canada! Your courage and the fact that you are so open to new ideas are inspiring. Thank you for supporting us in international waters.

Patrick Favre, Mr 1000 Volts! You support our French-speaking clients perfectly with great commitment, perseverance and energy. Thanks to you, there are no language barriers in our company. *Merci*, Patrick!

I would also like to thank all those whose example and experiences have helped me breathe life into the figure of Joe Friedmann.

About the author

Together with his business partner Jörg Neumann, Daniel Zanetti runs NeumannZanetti & Partner, a firm of consultants in Switzerland, founded in 1996. The company specializes in communication training, mystery checks and executive search. Its clients come from all over the world and from all branches.

Daniel Zanetti's core competence is in the fields of customer amazement, empowerment consultancy, staff motivation, management training and executive search.

In the field of customer amazement, he advises clients with tips on how to make their service stand out from the rest.

He is the initiator of the 'Joe Friedmann Customer Amazement Award' and the author of the bestseller *1001 Tips zur Mitarbeitermotivation (1001 Tips on Motivating Your Staff)*, published by Redline Wirtschaft in 2001.

Introduction

Do it big or stay in bed.

Larry Kelly

How are you?

'How are you?' the marketing manager of one of our customers asked me on the phone last year. 'I'm doing great!' I answered. 'Oh, come on!' she replied almost incredulously. I insisted that it was the honest truth. 'Everyone's complaining except you, apparently!' she said.

It's all a question of attitude. Of course I have my problems, too, my fears and worries. But nevertheless, the good things in life still far outnumber the bad!

For many months now, the papers have been full of pessimistic headlines. Rising unemployment, falling stock prices, companies merging and denying rumours of pending bankruptcy. Things are undoubtedly not what they used to be.

And under the weight of all this, a type of mass paralysis has begun to affect our society. You feel it when you phone someone for the first time. The obligatory opening question, 'How are you?' is usually followed by a sigh on the other end of the line.

What a dreadful frame of mind this reveals! The problems themselves are not the problem; it is the attitude of those who are supposed to solve them that is at fault. Our own personal take on life makes all the difference between happiness and unhappiness, and it plays a crucial role in customer relations.

Amazing your customers is not a new idea, nor do I claim to be its originator or have any ambition to go down in history as the inventor of this strategy. But it has been a way of life for me for many years now. It has brought me success, a success that, above all, has greatly enriched my life. If you pamper your customers, they in turn will pamper you, and suddenly a customer becomes more than just someone who owes you money.

Amazing my customers has become my passion, a passion that I would like to share with you. Read this book and let it inspire you. It is the result of personal experience, of things I have heard or learnt, but above all, its insights are tried and tested.

Every story told in this book is a true one. These are stories I, as its author, have either experienced myself or been told by others. The fact that these stories are all true is what really brings this book to life and makes it so relevant. And so I dedicate this book to all those whose positive experiences with the art of amazing customers have helped make this such an inspiring book.

If you let it, this book could be one of the best investments you have ever made. The choice is yours.

Oh, and by the way, 'How are you?'

1 Amaze your customers!

Joe Friedmann

I would like to start by introducing you to Mr Joe Friedmann. Joe represents us all in our role as customers. The stories in this book will often make you smile, and you will be able to identify with Joe, because his experiences are your experiences.

Joe Friedmann is sometimes the businessman and sometimes the father. He has his good days and his bad days. And like all of us, he lives his life as a customer. He earns money and he spends it.

Let Joe show you what everyday life as a customer is like. And go ahead: smile at all the bad examples. There are certainly enough of them around!

Yet there would be no credit in writing a book that simply shows how *not* to do it. Instead, I would like to offer a wealth of amazing examples that prove there is another way – a better and, as I like to call it, an amazingly good way!

The first chapter of this book offers an analysis of the way customers and suppliers of goods and services act at the moment. It includes a great variety of examples taken from everyday life. They illustrate how we customers experience services and how incredibly devoid of emotion our lives as customers actually are.

However, the true value of this book lies not in a theoretical treatment of the subject, but in the practical relevance of Chapter 2. In it, we take a look at Joe Friedmann's customer diary and enter a world that will be very familiar to you: the world of the customer. Joe describes his at times unbelievable and frustrating life as a customer, from his experiences as a patient on the dentist's chair to life as a hotel guest.

But don't worry. These alarming episodes are brief and each is followed by examples of amazingly good customer service we could all learn something from.

Satisfied is not satisfied enough

The idea for this book came to me almost eight years ago. My business partner Jörg Neumann and I had taken the plunge and set up in business on our own, and we were thinking about what sort of relationship we were aiming for with our customers.

One thing was clear from the start: as the owners of a company, we are interested in establishing long-term relationships with our customers. Another important point: we don't work for just anyone. That's right: not everyone can become one of our customers. That may sound arrogant, but in the end I am and always have been convinced that mutual liking accounts for 50 per cent of success.

And if success is 50 per cent attributable to mutual liking, then the other 50 per cent is performance. Service needs to be professional and of a high quality to ensure that customers are satisfied. But is keeping the customer satisfied enough? Is that a sufficient basis for long-term customer relations?

Isn't it a fact that customers take it for granted that you will render services professionally? And the bad news is: your customers probably won't even see your professionalism as anything special.

The goal is to have actively satisfied customers

Answer these questions intuitively, without long reflection:

Who do you bank with?

Name of the bank: _____

Why?

Reasons: _____

_____

_____

The passively satisfied customer

If no good reasons for having chosen your particular bank came to mind immediately, you can consider yourself a passively satisfied customer.

Typical reasons given by a passively satisfied customer would be:

- 'My parents banked their savings there.'
- 'I've banked with them for years and never had cause for complaint.' (But neither have you had cause for praise!)
- 'It's a well-known bank.'
- Or even: 'Actually, I don't really know why I chose that particular bank.'

The actively satisfied customer

- 'I have a very good relationship with the person who handles my account. He or she is always there when I need them and has always given me good advice.'
- 'My bank regularly arranges events to which I am invited, for example their annual golf tournament, theatre performances, etc.'
- 'My bank has excellent online-trading software that allows me to buy or sell stock from home.'

If you gave reasons like these, then you are an actively satisfied customer. There is a big difference!

You could say that passively satisfied customers become customers by accident. They will tend to change banks as soon as another bank offers them better conditions or an added advantage. They are easily persuaded to take their custom elsewhere. And as there is no bond between these customers and their bank, they will have no qualms about going elsewhere.

In contrast, actively satisfied customers can give good reasons for having chosen a particular bank. They are actively satisfied with the service provided and will say so whenever an opportunity presents itself. They can identify with the good service their bank provides. For them, it is unique!

But what if a company is not unique in any way? What if you discover that even though your company is running smoothly, your customers perceive it as boring?

> We are all both employees of a company and customers, so I would advise you to think about where you are a passively and where an actively satisfied customer. Think carefully before you decide where to buy and you will see that as an actively satisfied customer, you get more for your money!

Offer more than the customer expects

Many companies aim to do this. As it is a claim made in many company brochures, I would like to demonstrate briefly that this form of 'blowing your own trumpet' makes no sense whatsoever when seen from the customer's point of view.

It is a fact that requirements can vary greatly from customer to customer. One customer will place more value on the advice you have to offer, while for another, warranties and delivery periods are of more importance, and yet another will be mainly interested in your prices.

So if it is a company's declared aim to exceed the customer's expectations, it will first have to define exactly what each individual customer's expectations are. The only way to do this is to interview customers or have them fill out questionnaires. No problem for a firm of consultants doing the bulk of its business with just a hundred customers or clients, but what about a large-scale retailer or an insurance company with several thousand customers? There's no way such a company can do this, unless it manages to make itself amazingly unique!

The desperate quest for uniqueness

If you ask people what is special or unique about their company's products or services, you will usually see raised eyebrows:

- 'What's special or unique about ferrying someone from A to B in a taxi?'
- 'We're hairdressers. We cut hair.'

We have all taken a taxi or had our hair cut many times in our lives, so go ahead and relate a few astounding experiences you have had as a customer using these two services. You can't think of even one case where you were amazed? Don't worry! You're not the only one! *This book will change that!*

By the way: the next time you sit down on that hairdresser's chair, just ask yourself the following questions:

- 'What is unique about this hairdressing salon?'
- 'What do they offer that I can't get elsewhere?'
- 'What's the advantage for me in getting my hair cut here?'

Welcome to the emotionless world of the customer

Have you ever noticed how unemotional an experience spending money is? You get the same service almost everywhere and, even worse, it's predictable! Where can we still find the unusual? Where is the variety that is the spice of our life as a customer?

Increasingly, the retail trade is facing the problem of what it will have to offer its customers in future. We can choose between umpteen different TV channels, spend whole evenings zapping through the various forms of entertainment offered, only to go to bed at 11 o'clock, frustrated because we haven't really watched anything properly.

Or we are considering buying a new car and have to choose from a huge selection of colours and more than 40 different interior designs. Then we buy a car, and after only a year we face the frustration of seeing that there is already a whole new variety of innovative products and services available. Instead of better service, what customers are getting is a greater and greater number of interchangeable products.

Yet marketing managers spend a lot of time gathering information on their customers, information that, unfortunately, is seldom analysed and even more rarely put to any practical use to improve the service to the customer. This field of activity is called Customer Relations Management (CRM) and is implemented with the aid of a great deal of money and even more time in many companies. But what is the use of gathering all these data and storing them if they are not used to provide an even better service for the customer?

Your health insurance company is perfectly well aware that

you broke your leg in a skiing accident. They even know what hospital you are in. Yet none of its 5,000 employees sends you a 'Get Well Soon' card. When they do write to you, the first thing you will see, right at the top of the letter, is a multi-digit number. That number is you. A long, impersonal, meaningless number. And the letter doesn't start, 'Dear Joe Friedmann, We wish you a speedy recovery' and it isn't signed, 'Your health insurance team' either. No, it's a standard letter that begins, 'Dear customer' or even, 'Dear Sir/Madam'. And this is a company you may have been insured with for over 10 years! Yet another example of the failure of CRM.

So you see that although we are inundated with information and options, few companies ever seize the opportunity to offer an emotional experience, which to me is a very simple way to amaze your customers. It is no longer the product that is important, but how you handle it.

Customers are really hungry for those pleasing little experiences when they spend their money, and although everyone complains about unfriendly service and moans that businesses should be more customer-oriented, the situation doesn't really seem to be improving. And this has negative consequences, both for the customer and for the provider:

- Most consumers don't enjoy spending money any more. They go shopping because they have to and not because it's fun.

- Firms provide a service that leaves no lastingly positive impression with the customer. The consequences are fatal, since the customer defines you via your product and not your performance, and you can bet that the customer can get that same product from any other firm on the market in the same quality and at the same price.

I took a closer look at why we customers are only offered experiences that are devoid of any emotional component. In the following pages, I would like to share my insights with you.

A look in the rear-view mirror

Every day, you spend your hard-earned money on goods and services. And the shopping ritual follows the same pattern almost everywhere. This has one serious drawback, namely that a service is no longer perceived as such.

Look back over the last 24 hours and try to remember what you spent money on:

- Did you spend money 10 or even 20 times?

- Did you feel like a customer or more like you were begging?

- Which of the services you 'bought' came to mind immediately, and which can you hardly remember?

If you have difficulty remembering certain services you availed yourself of in the last 24 hours, then you were shopping on autopilot. Of course, this is not your problem, but the problem of the provider. A company should be aware how important it is that their customers buy a product or a service consciously. Of course, I don't only mean that you should be conscious of the product or the service itself, but above all of the way it is sold to you. Only if you consciously perceive the service as good will you be inclined to shop there again. This is the only way to establish a bond between a company and its customers.

Let me use an example to explain this. I bet you can predict exactly what will happen when you check in at your hotel, even before you set out on holiday. Make a note of what you think the check-in procedure will be.

Below you will see how similar your experiences are to my own. In my life, I have stayed in hotels more than a thousand times. And of those thousand experiences, I would only class 5 per cent as amazingly good. The rest have been wiped from my memory. Shame on me? No, shame on the hotels I have forgotten. They passed up the opportunity to make a lasting positive impression on me.

Ninety-five per cent of the time, this is what happens when you check in at a hotel:

1. You come through the door and enter the hotel lobby.

2. Behind a counter, you will find a receptionist. (Why behind a counter? Do you greet guests to your home from behind a counter?)

3. You will be welcomed more or less cordially.

4. Very probably you will be asked standard questions such as, 'Did you find your way here all right?' or, 'Was your trip ok?'

5. Then you enter your details on the appropriate registration form. They could quite easily spare you most of this (apart from signing the register), especially if they got the necessary information from you when you made your reservation.

6. Now the receptionist hands you the key to your room and gives you some information on when the hotel restaurant is open, the use of the hotel pool and instructions on how to get to your room, etc.

7. You cross the lobby to the lift, and you can read what happens next a few pages further on, in the story 'Make yourself at home'.

In most hotels, the ritual for welcoming guests has degenerated to a standard form, and the employees who welcome you are little more than dispensers of a mechanical notion of quality. This is the unfortunate result of standardization of service. We are no longer served spontaneously and individually, but by employees working by rote.

You will find the same applies when it comes to checking out. You approach the reception desk and tell the female clerk, who has her eyes firmly fixed on her computer monitor: 'I'd like to check out, please.' And without so much as a 'Good morning, Mr Friedmann. I hope you slept well?', she says: 'Did you have anything from the minibar, sir?' When you have guests staying at your home, do you greet them first thing in the morning with: 'Well, did you take anything from the fridge?'

The reason I'm emphasizing this so strongly is that nowadays, many hoteliers refer to themselves as your 'hosts'. But surely being a host means giving something to your guests, not robbing them of the feeling that they are welcome visitors.

There's no doubt about it: there are valuable opportunities being wasted here. And the hotel described here stands as just one example among hundreds of services provided to consumers in everyday life. Moreover, the poor service is not the result any of ill-will on the part of the employees, but of pure and simple thoughtlessness.

An astonishing metamorphosis – when a seller becomes a buyer

People tend to apply different yardsticks to their behaviour, and this is particularly true of sales people at the end of the working day, when they suddenly become customers rather than the providers of a service, as the following example shows.

An unfriendly shoe salesman finishes work at 6 pm and meets up with colleagues in a restaurant. In the course of their meal, he gets worked up because he finds the waitress unfriendly. Somewhere between 6 and 7 pm, this salesman has undergone an astonishing metamorphosis. Within the space of a mere 60 minutes, the salesman has become a customer.

On the other hand, in the lunchtime rush, a waitress may have difficulty getting the bill to a group of stressed-out managers on time. The guests are annoyed about this and don't tip very handsomely, which, in turn, gets her annoyed. When she finishes work at 2 pm, she goes to her bank, where she gets very impatient because she has to wait 10 minutes simply to place a standing order.

As customers, we expect quick, faultless and friendly service. Yet the moment we slip into our role as the providers of services, it's quite a different matter. We become extremely sensitive and take every piece of critical feedback from our customers as a personal insult. If only the providers of services treated their customers as they themselves would like to be treated, we would be living in a customer paradise!

They need to know you

'Do good and talk about it' is an old adage that, unfortunately, is seldom observed. If consumers don't know a company, they can't spend their money there. When you are thinking of buying a new car, you will choose from among the manufacturers you know. Tough luck for those manufacturers whose cars are less well known, but qualitatively just as good!

It follows that it is essential to make sure that consumers know your company. The media are, of course, an ideal way to do this, but there is one important consideration here: run-of-the-mill services will not attract media attention. So if you want your company to become a household name, you will have to offer something special, or journalists will never ask you for an interview, you will never smile into a TV camera, and never get the edge over your competitors.

There are two ways in which a provider can survive: either by being cheaper than the competition or by offering goods or services that are a cut above the rest.

As the quality of products in our Western markets is very high (they stopped making poor-quality cars in the 1980s), it follows that it is increasingly difficult to gain that competitive edge by offering better quality. It is far easier to be better by being 'different'. Once again, innovation is required. The only question is, where can we find that innovation?

See things through the eyes of your customers and be innovative!

Customers want good service, but they complain of getting

poor value for their money, unfriendliness, inefficiency, etc. Only by providing customer-oriented service will a company get its customers to perceive a service they would normally take for granted as something special. This gives a company several decisive advantages:

- The customer sees the price–performance ratio as positive. Where what they are getting is unique, consumers will no longer automatically draw comparisons with rival products and services.

- The customer is positively impressed with this special product or service and will automatically tell others about it, providing free advertising. Just think of it: your paying customer is at the same time helping you sell your products, free of charge. Wow!

- It gives your company an image boost. People will perceive you as innovative and better than your competitors.

- All these points will automatically result in increased consumer awareness of your company.

There are three reasons why most people are *not* innovative:

1. They lack the courage to be different.

2. They lack the talent for striking up friendly relationships with their customers.

3. They fail to put the knowledge they have to good use consistently.

But it doesn't have to be that way.

Courage, goodwill and consistency – an unbeatable trio

Where's your courage?

If there is one thing we lack today, it is courage. And when I say courage, I am not talking about performing a tightrope act without a safety net or skydiving. I mean the courage we all need in everyday business life, the courage to be different and to stand out from the rest of the field.

Just being different won't automatically make you better than your competitors, but it is often enough to give your company the reputation of being innovative. Be different and better, is the motto!

For example, when you ring a company and there is no one available immediately to take your call, you will almost certainly be asked to wait, with a canned version of Verdi's 'Four Seasons' playing in the background, or alternatively, a monotonous voice intoning the dreaded words, 'Please hold the line... Please hold the line... Please...'. Why not play a comedy CD instead, so that if your customers do have to wait, at least they will have something to laugh about?

In my company, we have been using a comedy CD for quite some time now to make waiting a more pleasurable experience for our customers, and quite a few companies have already copied the idea. Imitation is a form of flattery.

I admit that the idea might not exactly be ingenious, but it is certainly courageous. When I tell people about it, they can usually think of numerous reasons why this idea would not work in their particular company:

- 'That just wouldn't work in our branch!'
- 'Our customers might not take us seriously.'
- 'What if they don't like that particular comedian?' and so on and so forth.

They can come up with a host of arguments against the idea, but none in favour. What a fainthearted attitude that reveals. Just be like all the others, don't experiment, and never try anything new, because it might be a flop.

I would like to tell you another story on the subject of 'courage', one that really did happen.

One beautiful autumn day, I met Heinrich Gruben, the CEO of Hightech, for lunch. I was very proud that this top-shot manager had expressed an interest in our services, and I had done my homework thoroughly before this, our first meeting. After the usual words of welcome, the waiter handed us the menu and we both began to study it. Suddenly, Mr Gruben said 'Mmmm, they serve crêpes Suzette here!' (Crêpes Suzette are flambéed pancakes.) He didn't order them, however, despite his appreciative 'Mmmm'. Our lunch went well, but without any direct 'financial reward' for our company. When I arrived back in my office, I opened our Customer Loyalty System (we deliberately *don't* call it a database, as we don't see our clients as data to be managed) and typed in: 'Mr Gruben loves crêpes Suzette!'

And that, for the moment, was the end of the story. Nothing special. My notes only came into play about three months later. In mid-month, we always print out the list of clients who celebrate their birthdays in the following month. And one entry read, '15 January: Heinrich Gruben'.

In our company, I am the person responsible for the

implementation of our customer amazement strategy, and so it — was my job to decide whether we could amaze Mr Gruben and how. I switched on my computer and found various entries under 'Heinrich Gruben': address, position, phone number, comments. Under 'comments', I found the following:

- Dresses very elegantly.

- Smokes Davidoff cigarettes.

- Drives a roadster.

- Has two children (David, 6 and Lisa, 3).

- Wife, Anja, comes from Sweden.

And then, right at the bottom:

- *Loves crêpes Suzette.*

Three days before his birthday, I phoned Mr Gruben's secretary and asked whether he would be in his office on 15 January. She informed me that he would be in a company meeting until 3.30 pm and then in his office until about 5.30 pm. I thanked her, dialled the number of the restaurant we had had lunch at – it is not far from Mr Gruben's office – and gave the waiter the following instructions: 'On 15 January I would like you to take your flambé trolley to the company Hightech and serve crêpes Suzette in the office of its CEO, Mr Heinrich Gruben.' At first, the waiter thought I was someone from the local radio station playing a joke on him, but with the help of a 10-euro tip and my considerable powers of persuasion, I managed to talk him into carrying out this, as he put it, 'unusual order'.

I didn't have to wait long for a reaction. After carrying out my instructions, the waiter phoned me, bubbling over with enthusiasm, and told me what had happened. He created quite a stir from the moment he entered the reception area of the office building pushing the flambé trolley loaded with pans and all the necessary ingredients. 'Who do you want to see?' 'Where are you taking that?' 'To the boss?' Eventually, he entered the lift, pressed the button for the managers' floor and soon found himself face to face with an amazed Heinrich Gruben.

'Mr Gruben, I am here to wish you a very happy birthday on behalf of NeumannZanetti & Partner and to serve you your favourite dessert in honour of the occasion.'

Mr Gruben was so delighted that he called his colleagues in for an impromptu 'get together'. Over crêpes Suzette, they speculated about how NeumannZanetti & Partner could have known Mr Gruben's date of birth and what his favourite dessert was. Some of the employees themselves wouldn't even have known it was his birthday if it hadn't been for our little surprise, let alone that he liked flambéed pancakes. (The answer is, of course, we acquired our information through active listening!)

The following week, we received a page-long letter from Mr Gruben describing how delighted he had been with our birthday gift. I really had succeeded in amazing this client, and years later, people would still ask me about it. Today, Hightech is one of our clients and Mr Gruben more than just another business associate.

The question I would like to ask you is: was this particularly courageous of me? The answer is: *no!*

It was not courageous, because I wasn't just guessing that Heinrich Gruben loved crêpes Suzette: *I knew!* If it had been just guesswork, I might have been wrong, and then the whole operation could have been a flop. But since I knew he was partial to crêpes, I didn't need courage. All I had to do was to put my knowledge to good use. And by the way, the whole campaign cost my company just 30 euros, including the 'bribe' for the waiter.

What would have been the alternatives:

- a bouquet of flowers for 30 euros?

- a bottle of wine for 20 euros?

- no birthday present at all?

Decide for yourself whether it was worth it and how effective our little surprise was.

All successful companies demonstrate courage. You can't be innovative without taking risks. If you aren't innovative, customers will avoid you. And when customers avoid you, your company goes down the drain.

Dale Carnegie, asked about the motto of his life, once said: 'Make a fool of yourself, every day!' A motto well worth taking to heart, don't you think?

Goodwill, or mutual liking

It is mutual liking that ensures that customers identify emotionally with a person, a product or a brand. It is mutual liking that compels us to return to a restaurant where we are on first-name terms with the waiter and where we can expect good service.

Mutual liking makes it a little easier for us to spend our money. We are inclined to be more generous to people who are friendly and, above all, our level of tolerance is higher when others are friendly. Even if mistakes are made, we remain calm and collected, provided that we like those we are dealing with. And it cannot be denied that it is a mutual liking that leads us to fall in love. Friendly and pleasant people are more attractive. They radiate warmth, energy and an aura of success.

If you want to buy a new car, you can choose between hundreds of dealers. If you compare, you will see that prices, even for a new car, do vary considerably. By haggling with the dealer, you can almost always knock the price down to the level of the cheapest dealer. But the question is: which dealer will you buy your car from if the price is the same everywhere? The answer is: from the one you like best!

In other words, what we need today is not experts on prices and policies, but experts on dealing with people. Why should you hand over your money to someone who is rude, is not interested in your needs and doesn't even pronounce your name properly? To someone who is badly dressed and has no manners?

If you have courage, and if you genuinely like people, there's just one more thing you need to make you an innovative amazer of your customers: consistency.

Consistency

Consistency is what you need to pursue your goal unwaveringly.

Recently, a shoemaker who makes orthopaedic footwear told me how delighted his customers are when he phones them about three weeks after they purchase shoes from him and inquires whether their new shoes are comfortable and whether there is anything else he can do for them. His customers are completely amazed by so much customer-orientation and tell him that hardly anyone bothers to inquire how satisfied they are once a sale is completed.

Well, this shoemaker has proved that he has the courage to be different, and it is certainly a very kind gesture, but it is a pity that he doesn't follow through and extend the same courtesy to all his clients. He told me that he only has time to contact about 30 per cent of his customers.

He is full of enthusiasm and proud of the success of this measure, which brings him a lot of trade as his customers recommend him to friends and acquaintances. Yet at the same time, he confessed that his business is struggling.

I am firmly convinced that he should extend this service to all his clients, as this would bring him even more satisfied customers who would advertise actively for his business. The question is not how much time something takes or how much it costs. The only legitimate question is: what's in it for the customer?

A matter of timing

Amazing your customers requires careful timing. You want the positive effect for your customer to be as lasting as possible. So the question is: what is the best time to stage your little surprise?

For example, while talking to one of your customers, you hear that he is to deliver an important speech before an audience of clients. This is the sort of thing likely to make anyone slightly nervous and anxious to make a good impression.

You have come up with the idea of surprising your customer with a can of 'Red Bull' and a book entitled 'Top Quotes from Top Public Speakers'. A hand-written card with the following words of encouragement will accompany the gift: '... gives you power and lends your words wings. With best wishes for a successful speech, from...'.

The parcel is to be delivered by post. When do you think would be the ideal time for your customer to open this parcel:

- two to three days before he is due to give the speech?
- the day before?
- on the day itself?

Psychologically, the ideal timing would be for the parcel to arrive two to three days before your customer is due to deliver his speech, first, because your customer can appreciate its symbolic value longer, right up to the moment of truth, and secondly because this will give him time to find some great quotes for his speech in the book you are enclosing.

Put yourself in your customer's shoes for a moment, and imagine what you would think if you were the recipient of this surprise parcel. Wouldn't your thoughts run along these lines:

- 'How nice of him to think of me!'
- 'Amazing that he found the time to go to such trouble, even though he must be an extremely busy man!'
- 'Wow, he really knows how to motivate people!'
- 'I ought to think up something like that for my customers!'

You will see that instead of merely identifying yourself with your own achievements, you are identifying yourself with the person who sent you this 'amazing' gift! Follow the example and be unforgettable for your customers! Discover the brand 'Me'!

The brand 'Me'

The art of amazing your customers as I define it is an attitude, even a philosophy. If you live and breathe this type of relationship with your customers, you are sure to enjoy an excellent reputation with them. People will speak positively of you and you will become a brand. A unique and distinctive brand. You will no longer need titles on your business card because your name will speak for itself.

(I have never understood why so many people feel the need to point out what they do or who they are on their business cards. If a customer doesn't notice, doesn't feel *what* or *who* you are, you might as well forget it right away.)

On your way to becoming the brand 'Me' it might be a good idea to ask yourself the following questions, and it would be nice if you could answer them all intuitively with a firm yes:

- If I were a waiter or waitress, would I like to be served by me?

- Do I consider myself a good person?

- Do I often make others laugh?

- Do I sometimes do things that are 'simply not done'?

- Do people I have regular contact with immediately recognize my name?

- Do I often receive gifts? Even from my own customers?

- Am I really passionate about my work?

- Would I feel easy if all my customers were gathered together in one room?

Don't forget to listen

We live in a society in which few people have the gift of being good listeners. So it is hardly surprising that many salespeople forget to switch their ears to receiving mode when they are talking to their customers. They are so preoccupied with thinking, 'I have to close a deal,' that they are more concerned with themselves than with the other person.

Listening is a sign of esteem and of respect. If we don't listen, we can hardly hope to understand others. But above all, listening is clever. I personally get some of my best ideas for amazing my customers by actively listening to them.

Listening actively also helps to avoid misunderstandings. Listening actively means signalling our understanding. Repeating what we have heard and dealing with open questions that turn up in the course of a conversation are signs that we are listening actively. Body language signals such as nodding and an open body stance actively support this.

By nature, of course, salespeople will be better talkers than listeners. All the more reason for them to try to improve their listening skills. Immediately before sales talks, they should try to 'anchor' the following thought in their minds: 'I know I'm a good talker. With Mr Smith, I am going to be a good listener, too!'

Afterwards, in order to test whether they have been

listening actively, sales personnel with an earnest desire to become better listeners can ask themselves the following questions:

- What names did my customer mention in the course of our conversation?

- What figures or sums were mentioned?

- What does my customer expect me to do next?

- Did he or she appear to be under stress?

- How good is my customer feeling, on a scale of 1 to 10?

Critical questions on customer amazement strategies

People often ask me the following three questions on the subject of my customer amazement strategy:

Question 1. From a hotel manager

'Customers today expect more and more. If I amaze my customers, next time they come they will expect to be amazed again. How can I meet ever-higher expectations?'

The bad news first: innovation is not a one-off thing! You can't afford to amaze your customers and then rest on your laurels. Today's laurels will be on the compost heap tomorrow!

Offering your customers an unusual service is not something that is prescribed, but a question of culture. See your customers' expectations as a challenge and not as a threat.

Question 2. From a travel agency employee

'*I had the idea of sending all customers who booked a holiday in the sun with us a tube of sun-tan lotion with a corresponding sun protection factor before their departure. But what if the customer doesn't want to be amazed? What if he or she doesn't like surprises? What if he or she has already bought sun-tan lotion for their holiday?*'

Anyone who asks questions like this is making two important mistakes. First, these questions reveal a lack of courage and consistency. If this employee never tries out the idea, he will never find out whether his customers would have liked the idea. And the customer, on the other hand, will never feel the need to thank him for this friendly gesture, because, thanks to a lack of courage and consistency, they never had the chance to enjoy this unusual service.

Secondly, you will never find out whether your idea for amazing your customers would have worked if you never try it out.

Question 3. From a car salesman

'*I think the idea of amazing your customers is a good one, but I simply don't have the time to do it. I have so many appointments every day that I'm just too busy to work out strategies like that. How can I find the time to amaze my customers?*'

This is quite simply a lame excuse. I will say it once again: the question everyone has to ask himself or herself is: *What benefits does my customer amazement strategy have for my customer?* Read on to the end of the book and decide for yourself!

And, if I may be allowed one final question, *What benefits does it have for me?*:

- If I give to my customers by amazing them, could it be that I will then get more in return?

- Won't I rise in their esteem?

- Won't this make me special and especially successful?

- Couldn't it also bring increased job satisfaction for me?

The only way to find out is by trying it! And today is the perfect day to start. Believe me, there is never a better day than today. Now or never!

Your customers will never forget you for it.

2 Joe Friedmann's amazing experiences as a customer

Make yourself at home

Make yourself at home, it says on the front of the hotel brochure I am skimming through, balancing it on my knees between my palmtop and my briefcase on the worn back seat of a taxi. We are all cosmopolitan nowadays. Far from being pure luxury, it's a necessary evil for many businesspeople. The great thing about travelling, you might think, is that you get to see something new. Then where on earth did they get the idea that I want everything in my hotel to be just like it is at home?

An almost smiling receptionist, who, as far as I can see, consists of just a head and an upper torso, greets me from behind the desk. The sign in front of her '*Inge – Front Office Assistant*' tells me her first name, but somehow I haven't the courage to address her by it. Elegantly sliding the registration form across the counter towards me, she asks me whether I found my way to the hotel all right. What a question! *Make yourself at home,* it says on the sign next to the lift. Personally, I never welcome guests to my home from behind a desk, nor do I expect them to fill out a registration form the minute they come through the door. As a host, I would never be so impersonal.

'Please follow me,' says Inge as we step out of the lift on the third floor. I travel a lot, and in eight hotels out of ten I am welcomed and shown to my room by a receptionist in this same stereotyped manner. I am just wondering whether Inge is going to be an exception, but no. She, too, shows me where the minibar is. Even worse, she shows me where the bathroom is. Do I look such an idiot in my suit and with my briefcase that she thinks I won't be able to find the minibar and the bathroom in this tiny, 20-square-metre room? For the umpteenth time, I am subjected to this humiliating ritual. And she hasn't finished yet. She also draws the fruit bowl and the bottle of mineral water to my attention, both generously included in the price of the room. 'I hope you have a pleasant stay,' says Inge, now sounding slightly stressed, while her bleeper alerts her to the arrival of another guest.

Before I go to sleep, I want to make some notes and decide to do so in the comfort of the bed. As I get in, I see the chocolate heart that has been placed on the pillow. What a pity I've just cleaned my teeth.

I could have written my notes on the desk, of course, but unfortunately, the hotel team has decided to use it as a display area for menus, a selection of brochures, a bottle opener, an ashtray, etc. One glance at the contents of the drawer reveals that the Bible remains untouched by anyone except the person who placed it there, a relic of times long past and a pitiful sign of a lack of innovation on the part of the hotel management.

Make yourself at home, I think as I fall asleep.

What is wrong with the tourist trade? Has no one ever thought of seeing things from the point of view of the customer and trying to inject a little customer-orientation into the proceedings? Innovation sounds good as long as you're not expected to practise it.

Amazingly good!

A hotel in Sydney asks its guests when they check in: 'Would you like a goldfish in your room?' Guests can choose a fish at the reception desk and have it placed in their room in an aquarium.

The 'March of the Ducks' has become the hallmark of a hotel in Orlando, Florida. Twice a day, the ducks march along a red carpet from the hotel fountain through the reception area and back. Ducks have played a historical role here for decades and are 'sacred' animals. You can find them as a motif all over the hotel, from the duck-shaped pats of butter on the dining table to the soap in your room. And it goes without saying that you won't find duck anywhere on the menu.

At a hotel in the canton of Ticino in Switzerland, guests check in not at a counter, but sitting on comfy armchairs and sofas. The receptionist first offers them a drink and then takes care of the formalities. And the guests are not expected to fill out the registration form themselves. The receptionist does it for them. A far more pleasant way to start your stay in a hotel.

Instead of the usual Bible, a hotel in Zurich places a book with the intriguing title, *Are You Good in Bed?* in its rooms. It is so popular that guests often ask to buy copies!

A hotel in England had an idea to make dogs feel welcome. On arrival, your four-footed companion receives a gift package including a squeaky toy and dog biscuits. The hotel also has a dog bowl with your dog's name on it, a woven dog basket with a pocket for bones and a metal nameplate with the logo of the hotel. The hotel also provides a map of the surroundings with ideas for interesting walks. And of course, all hotel employees address your dog by name.

No overhead projector required

As I frequently attend seminars and also conduct them myself, I know many seminar hotels all over the world. However, most hotels award themselves the title 'seminar hotel' all too glibly, as the following story shows.

It is 11 pm in Zurich when I turn into the drive of the hotel where I will be holding a two-day seminar. 'You can't leave your car here, sir,' are the welcoming words I get from an over-zealous porter. 'And a very good evening to you, too,' I reply, hoping he will realize how rude he has been. No chance.

After eventually finding a parking space, I am standing at the reception desk reading the hotel brochure because the receptionist is still talking on the phone. *Our ultramodern rooms all have a TV/radio, shower/bath and direct outward dialling.*

Incredible! I must have made a mistake. *Direct outward dialling!* In this day and age, in which every year two new mobile phone generations appear on the market and where every business-person carries a mobile, this hotel is proud of itself for offering its guests direct outward dialling. Welcome to the 21st century, is all I can say.

'Would you just fill in the hotel registration form, please?' says the receptionist. 'Do I really have to fill in all these details yet again?' I ask, somewhat irritated. 'It's not the first time I've stayed here, and I gave you all my details when I booked. You already have all the information required for the form.' 'I'm sorry, but we have our instructions,' replies my late-night adversary. And while I write 'secret agent' in the box marked 'Profession' and 'Highway to Hell' in the box for 'Street', I swear this will be the last time I hold one of my seminars in this hotel.

Whenever I conduct a seminar, I arrive the evening before, and for good reason! Now I ask the receptionist if I can put the material for my seminar in the room where it is to be held. 'What, now?' she asks reproachfully. 'Yes, now,' I answer in a friendly but firm tone. And when the porter unlocks the door to the room for me, the problems start. The room has not been arranged as I requested. Instead of a horseshoe-shaped arrangement of tables for 12 people, there is a block of tables for 16. And then there's the problem with the overhead projector. As I never use one for any of my seminars, my assis-tant always informs the hotel in writing that 'no overhead projector will be required'. But believe it or not, 60 per cent of the time there will be an overhead projector in the room, and I'm sure of my figures because I have to complain about it so often.

The person responsible will not be on duty until 8 o'clock the next morning, which means that I, the customer, have to roll up my sleeves and get cracking. I have to unplug the projector, move it to the side of the room out of the way, fold up the screen that goes with it and move the block of tables into a horseshoe arrangement – and only then can I set out my material for the seminar.

'Good morning, Mr Friedmann! Is everything to your satisfaction?' The young lady in charge of seminar organization at the hotel beams at me. I consult my watch. It is 7.55 am. My seminar starts at 8.30, which means that the first participants could be arriving any minute now.

I tell the seminar organizer that I had to put in a night shift. Of course, she is very sorry. Of course the booking confirmation on her clipboard says, 'no overhead projector required' and that I want the tables arranged in a horseshoe shape for 12 people. But unfortunately, the staff at this hotel, like that at so many others, are better at playing tennis (hitting the ball backwards and forwards over the net, putting the blame on the others) than at football (working together as a team to get the ball in the goal).

'Would you like a cup of coffee?' she asks me apologetically yet at the same time highly motivated. I say thanks, but no, as the first participant for my seminar arrives at that very moment. 'But there is one thing you could get me,' I whisper to her. 'Yes?' she asks. 'A wastepaper basket.'

In my experience, a wastepaper basket is missing from seminar rooms just as frequently as an unwanted overhead projector is found there.

Amazingly good!

One hotel specializing in catering for conferences and organized events offers an interactive room planner on its website home page. Clients can use it to plan events in the comfort of their own homes. It is user-friendly and functional.

These are my experiences at one seminar hotel that is truly worthy of the name. When I first consulted them on the subject of my seminar, they asked me exactly what the seminar was about, who would be participating, etc. Then they made a note of my wishes concerning furnishing and special equipment in the room, labels and nameplates, etc. The very next day, they e-mailed me a digital photograph of 'my' seminar room with the infrastructure and labels I had ordered. The reference line of the e-mail read: 'Dear Mr Joe Friedmann, is this the set-up you want?' I answer that it is exactly in accordance with my wishes, and the very next day, I get the confirmation of my booking in the post. And on the day of the seminar, I find the room exactly as it was shown on the photo.

In another hotel, the seminar organization team follows through by sending someone from the hotel to the seminar leader once the guests have left to inquire: 'Was your seminar a success? Let me offer you a drink, and later, someone will be along to help you clear up and pack.'

A little 'light' refreshment?

In the previous section, I described my experiences with conducting seminars, but you would be amazed at what you have to contend with as a participant.

I attend a week-long management seminar entitled 'Management through emotional competence'. It is 8 o'clock in Bavaria and I enter the seminar hotel where the event is due to begin at 9 am. At the reception desk, I introduce myself and explain that I will be participating in the seminar. 'Your room isn't free yet,' the receptionist says, though I haven't even inquired about my room. 'Actually, I just wanted to ask where the seminar is being held.'

'Let me look that up for you,' the employee says. She is dressed in a uniform in the colours of the hotel logo, and she begins to hammer away at the keyboard of her computer. While she is doing this, I look around the lobby, and my eyes are drawn to a board on which all the events taking place that day are listed. The last entry but one reads:

Seminar: Management through emotional competence.

And on the line beneath it says:

Franz Josef Room.

'In our Franz Josef Room,' I hear the receptionist say. Well done! She has now managed to find the information that is plain for all to see on a board not 15 yards from where she is sitting.

The seminar has begun and I look down at the notepad in front of me and see, in elegant lettering: '*We recommend our hotel for seminar events of all kinds.*'

Strictly speaking, I think to myself, it should be the guests who recommend a hotel and not the hotel itself singing its own praises, but that's another story. At 10.30 am, the drama 'Coffee break, part 1 of 10' begins. In a badly lit, stuffy corridor, we find the following arranged for us on a little trolley:

- a thermos flask of coffee;

- a thermos flask of hot water for tea;

- orange juice;

- spring water;

- tea bags;

- croissants;

- milk, sugar and sweeteners.

At 4.30 in the afternoon, we find almost precisely the same refreshments, only this time, there is cake instead of croissants.

The reason why I describe this as a drama is that in that week, we had a total of 10 coffee breaks, all with exactly the same refreshments and served in exactly the same location. The hotel is situated in such beautiful surroundings, and yet none of their overworked employees thought of serving the refreshments outside in good weather, or in one of the suites (which would at the same time have been good advertising for the hotel), in the hotel kitchen, as a power break with various fruit juices, as a chance to taste different teas, etc.

You don't have to be a creative genius to come up with 10 different ideas. All you need is a little more customer-orientation. The problem is that the seminar manager of this hotel hadn't taken part in a seminar himself in years and so had no idea what his seminar customers might appreciate.

The same can be said of the chef, who served up three-course meals with Bavarian dumplings every day, meals so heavy that we were in danger of falling asleep during the afternoon sessions. Seminar participants would much rather have a lunchtime buffet where they can choose individually how much and what they would like to eat.

On the second morning, still reeling from the chef's concerted attack on our digestive systems, we meet at the breakfast buffet. In a prominent position over the table, there hangs a carved wooden sign that reads:

> *A very good morning to all our guests!*
> *We hope you enjoy our rich breakfast buffet.*

We exchange looks and think to ourselves that we would rather have a more balanced breakfast than a rich breakfast buffet.

Amazingly good!

In a country hotel I once stayed at, an apprentice sliced and served exotic and local fruits at coffee time. This very welcome vitamin shot served two purposes: on the one hand, it was a valuable training exercise for the apprentice, and on the other, it guaranteed a pleasant and animated coffee break.

Another hotel has made catering for coffee breaks its speciality. The hotel team ensures that the participants in a seminar are served different refreshments in a different location in the hotel at every break. And so you will sometimes find top managers sitting cross-legged in the children's clubroom, playing with Lego and eating their cake.

With the compliments of the chef

'Name?' 'Friedmann. I booked a table two weeks ago,' I tell the head waiter, who is disguised as the perfect officer and gentleman. He clicks the nib of his cheap plastic biro in and out as he scans the pages of illegible entries in his thick reservations book in search of my name. I would have preferred to be greeted with a 'Welcome' or, 'Good evening, madam, sir.' After all, tonight is not just any old night. Tonight I'm taking the woman of my dreams out. But it doesn't look as though it's going to be a dream evening.

Once the other guests have had ample opportunity to give us the once-over, the head waiter finally manages to read his own handwriting, leads us to our table and immediately presents us with two bulky menus. 'The wine list' he adds and places this five-page Bible on my side of the table.

Just as I am starting a conversation with my companion, a nervous-looking young man appears at our table and asks, 'Bread?' Once we have each selected one of the 13 different sorts of bread available, I want to resume our conversation, but I can't for the life of me remember what it was I had been about to ask my girlfriend. We have just begun to chat about something else when the officer and gentleman turns up at our table again. His eyes firmly fixed on the pad in his hand, he scribbles something (probably our table number), then raises his gaze and peers at us over the edge of his glasses, though it looks more like he is raising his eyebrows, and asks, 'Are you ready to order?' Of course we are neither ready to order nor are we feeling very much at ease. Some strange sort of stress transference is taking place. People keep approaching our table with new offers: 'Mineral water?' 'Butter?' 'Have we taken your order?' It seems impossible that we are ever going to be able to have a private conversation.

'Why do you keep whispering?' 'I don't know,' I whisper back. What I do know, on the other hand, is exactly what is going to happen in the next few minutes. I know with absolute certainty that a waiter is going to approach our table with two plates of appetizers we have not ordered and present them with the words: 'With the compliments of the chef!' In such restaurants, I always bet with my colleagues that this will happen, and believe me, I always win! Someone must have invented the phrase, and as they are so innovative in the catering business, it is shamelessly copied all over the country.

'How would you like your tournedos, sir?' the waiter asks automatically when I order my main course. But no one asked me whether I would like the lamb carpaccio on mustard shoots that are presented 'with the compliments of the chef'. As I look around the restaurant, I see a mixture of guests – business-people, families, couples – but they all receive exactly the same treatment, although I would have thought that their requirements could not have been more different.

Exasperated when the waiter nips my declaration of love in the bud for the third time, I ask for the bill and spend more time waiting for and paying it than we have taken to eat our entire meal. We get into my car, deposit the menthol sweets they brought with the bill in the ashtray and drive home. No one disturbs us by playing a lacklustre version of 'New York, New York' for the second time, no one interrupts us to inquire 'Dessert?' A soft 'ding-dong' tells me that the frozen raspberries in the microwave are defrosted. And the two of us stand in the kitchen enjoying our vanilla ice cream with warm raspberries. And suddenly I remember what it was I had been going to ask the love of my life three hours previously.

Amazingly good!

In a Zurich restaurant, guests are asked when they book a table,

'How much time do you have for your lunch?' The waiter then guarantees that they will get the bill on time and won't have to wait another 20 minutes. This is particularly helpful for businesspeople who don't have much time to spare.

At a US restaurant chain, you can place a sign on the table signifying that you are ready for the next course or would like the bill.

Another restaurant confirms bookings via SMS: 'We look forward to welcoming you as our guest this evening. We have reserved a table for four for you at 8 pm.'

'A table for two for breakfast, please,' I requested when I checked in at my hotel. When the waiter showed us to our table the next morning, we found a card that read: 'We have the pleasure of reserving this table for Joe Friedmann and Ralph Hubacher, two gentlemen who know that a successful day begins with a good breakfast.'

In the United States, I met a very special waiter. He has noticed that many of the coats that the guests hand to him have torn hang loops. Whenever he can spare the time, he has taken to sewing these loops back on with thread of the appropriate colour. Not everyone notices, but those guests who do tell others about it. What exceptional service!

I could hardly believe my eyes when I walked onto the terrace of a restaurant in the mountains and found a set of binoculars on every table. The manager approached our table and said: 'Please do feel free to enjoy our breathtaking view. On your tablemats, you will find a map of the whole region to help you identify the landmarks you can see.'

A restaurant in Honolulu catering mainly to businesspeople has special white paper tablecloths on which guests can take notes over their lunch and then take them back to the office. This would be a great idea for family restaurants, too.

A restaurant in Cologne offers its customers a time guarantee: if the lunchtime meal they order is not on the table in 15 minutes, the guests get their meal free of charge.

Taxi!

Not: 'Good afternoon! Nice to have the pleasure of driving you!' And not: 'Good afternoon! Where would you like to go?' Whenever I take a taxi, the first thing I see is a bored, demotivated expression. As a customer, you get the impression you are disturbing the taxi driver, who would much rather go on reading his newspaper. And when the driver finally deigns to look at me, I am expected to state my destination. Such rude treatment makes me want to reply: 'Sorry, for a moment, I thought this was a taxi.' Instead, the taxi driver asks 'Where to?' and I say where I want to go, but instead of a friendly 'Certainly, sir!' in reply, I usually hear... absolutely *nothing*! I'm never sure whether the driver has really understood me or whether he is stepping on the gas in an automatic reflex. Perhaps, I think to myself, it's the end of his shift and he's driving home, not even realizing that he's got a fare.

As a businessman, I have often wondered where the management is here. Doesn't any taxi company give a jot how its drivers behave or about their personal hygiene? I can't imagine what criteria an applicant has to fulfil to get a job as a taxi driver, and surely my question is more than justified when you consider the great responsibility a taxi driver bears.

If ever there was a trade where good manners have gone to the dogs, it's this one. Drivers never ask whether I like the music that's playing. After all, I'm not a guest, just an annoying disturbance. They expect me to climb into a taxi that reeks of cigarette smoke without complaint. You can see how deep-seated my frustration is, and if I hadn't had the good fortune to experience really excellent service from a few taxi drivers, I could quite happily wish them all on the moon.

And it's particularly bad in tourist cities. At the station, you see huge signs that read '*Welcome to...*', but you only have to turn your head 180 degrees to see tourists heaving their own heavy cases into the boots of taxis while ill-bred taxi drivers stand by and watch. It's also a fact that most taxis in Europe look boring. In New York or London, tourists have their pictures taken standing next to taxis. Taking a taxi is one of the highlights of their holiday. Of course I realize that these people are in holiday mood and that it is in part the attraction of the exotic. But still, in many places we take a taxi because we have to, not out of choice. And the way most taxi drivers behave, that's not likely to change any time soon.

Amazingly good!

A friendly lady taxi driver in Frankfurt was happy to recommend a hotel that suited my budget. As my mobile needed recharging, she got the taxi company switchboard to find out the number of the hotel and lent me her own private mobile phone so that I could call them.

An older taxi driver in Düsseldorf welcomed me as if I were an old friend, held the door open for me, asked me for my destination, offered me his newspaper and addressed me by name when I got out. He handed me his business card, and it goes without saying that I booked my taxi for the return journey with the same company.

Once I visited a customer on my way to the airport in Chicago. I asked the taxi driver to wait for a few minutes. While he was waiting, he must have replaced the cheap plastic labels on my luggage. Unfortunately, I didn't notice this until I picked up my luggage at the baggage reclaim in Zurich.

Japanese taxi drivers give their passengers a very different welcome, with a friendly smile and spotlessly clean cars. They wear white gloves and nameplates, which shows their positive attitude to their job. They inquire what music the passengers would like to hear and provide brochures and cinema and restaurant tips. They distribute prepaid, addressed praise/criticism cards, stamped with the name of the driver and the taxi number so the guest can provide feedback on the quality of the service received. You see, there is another way!

Coffee, tea, mineral water, Coke, sandwiches

'Coffee, tea, mineral water, Coke, sandwiches!' Whenever I hear these words on a train, I automatically start grabbing deep breaths, because I know, as sure as the train's arrival and departure times, that 'he' is going to smell of sweat. Knowing what's coming, I hold my breath until he has gone past. 'He' is the waiter, and when he arrives I always have the same two choices: either I can opt for a session of intensive lung training (my record for holding my breath stands at 51 seconds) or subject my olfactory organ to an endurance test under extreme conditions.

'A ham sandwich, please.' Abruptly, I break off my lung training – my hunger is stronger than my need for fresh air. 'Ham sandwich-a is-a sold out,' the waiter replies, his face unmoved. With his left hand, he casually grasps the luggage rack above my head and thus transports me firmly and irrevocably to the land of unlimited odours.

'Well...' I begin hesitantly, trying not to breathe in further than is absolutely necessary, 'What else is there?' 'Coffee, tea, mineral water, Coke, sandwiches!' he answers promptly, while staring disinterestedly out of the window. I'm already getting irritated looks from the other passengers, so I jump up, grab the first sandwich that comes to hand and give him his four euros.

The sandwich is ice-cold and dried up, and it tastes ice-cold and dried up too, even though the recipe is actually so simple:

Quality + Friendliness = Success

Not all waiters on our trains have deodorants and selling skills. And they skimped on their training, too, if their attitude to their job is anything to judge by.

My bladder feels close to bursting, but although I really do desperately need to go, I check my watch. Perhaps I can hang on until I get to my destination; then I won't have to use the toilet on the train. There's nothing I hate more. From the overall colour scheme to the toilet bowl itself, the key design statement on trains is 'dingy'. The chances of finding a clean toilet are approximately zero, though in fact, all the designer had to do was to combine the practical with the aesthetically pleasing. And of course, they should clean the toilets more often. A company's toilets are its calling card, they say. Well, I assume the railway company must be clean out of calling cards...

'Tickets, please!' calls a ticket inspector who reminds me of an officer I met while doing military service. Laden with all the utensils of his job, he passes through the corridor, feet splayed to help him keep his balance in the swaying train. It's a soul-manager I need more than a corporal here.

'Zurich – end of the line! Passengers are asked to leave the train. See the information boards for connecting services!' Gee, thanks for telling me. I was feeling so comfortable there, I might almost have forgotten to get off.

Now, where's the nearest toilet?

Amazingly good!

A waiter on a train in Africa pushed his trolley cheerfully through the compartment, greeting each guest with a few friendly words. One passenger was eating a sandwich he had brought with him. The waiter gave him a serviette and wished him a pleasant journey. When he had moved on to the next compartment, the passengers all commented on how pleasant this young man was. When he passed through the compartment again 30 minutes later, almost everyone bought something from him. Being friendly does pay off!

In Indonesia, rail operators installed TV sets in the first-class compartments ten years ago.

In South Africa, the guard distributes the daily newspapers, as they do in airlines. In my opinion, this makes much more sense than printing a railway company magazine that hardly anyone reads anyway.

In Zurich, one woman discovered a niche in the market with her 'Coffee blitz'. Every morning she offers travellers on the municipal railway network fresh home-brewed coffee from a specially constructed canister she carries on her back.

35,000 euros – and no takers

It's Sunday, and I'm doing what I always do on Sundays, namely reading the newspapers. Like most people, I skip the adverts, and rarely does one ever catch my eye. But today is different, and it's all my girlfriend's fault. 'We need a bigger car, one where we don't have to take the pram apart every time we need to take it with us.' 'Sounds like we need a people carrier,' I reply, sighing mentally. I've never seen a people carrier I like. And just as my girlfriend repeats that we really do need a bigger car, my eye falls upon a picture of an aesthetically pleasing people carrier in my Sunday newspaper. It's a full-page advert with a freephone number in large print next to the words: *Call today and reserve your car for a test drive.* I tear the advert out and resolve to phone them from my office the next day.

'Welcome to AutoVan. My name is Cerutti. How may I help you?'

'Hello. I read your advertisement and would like some information about the new VanXL.'

'What would you like to know, sir?'

'How much does it cost, how long are delivery times and where is my nearest dealer?'

'One moment, please.' (We all know a moment can last an eternity, and in my case it's a full three minutes.)

'I'm sorry, sir. This is the call centre in Italy. All I can tell you is that prices start from about 20,000 euros. I'm afraid I don't have any other details.'

'Could you at least send me a brochure?'

'What, from Italy?'

I consult the phone directory on my computer and get the

numbers of three AutoVan dealers in my area. I phone all three and ask them to send me sales literature, as I am thinking of buying a car from them. Two of them never send me anything, let alone call me back.

'Darling, is our economy in recession or is it booming?' 'Why do you ask?' 'Oh, no particular reason.'

Three days later, I find the brochures from the third dealer in my letterbox. Wow, I think as I skim through them. The Italians really know how to appeal to the emotions, especially when it comes to cars. On the last page, I find the following text: '*The green number – one number is all you need for our extensive range of services.*' The number given is that of the call centre I phoned days before. Exactly the same number as in the advert. Oh well, things like that happen, I think.

The brochure also says in bold print that I should test-drive the VanXL before I buy. '*We will bring the VanXL to your home, provided you live not more than 50 kilometres from your registered dealer. On arrangement, you can test-drive the VanXL for a whole weekend.*'

Great, I think, and phone the dealer, full of anticipation about getting my test drive at last. 'Er... I'm only a grade B dealer, and I don't have a VanXL here [although the advert said the van is *available immediately from your AutoVan dealer*]. But I can give you the number of a grade A dealer. I know he has one,' the voice on the phone tells me. Ok, who cares, grade A or grade B, I just want to see this car.

When I finally get hold of the grade A dealer, he is quite rude: 'Why should I let you test-drive a VanXL for a whole weekend? Do you think I'm stupid, or what?' Dear reader, read on to the end of this story and you will see just how stupid he really is.

'Because it says so on the last page of the official brochure,' I reply and, just to make sure I haven't got it wrong: 'You are an authorized AutoVan dealer?'

'I don't care what it says in the brochure. The people who write the brochures don't run car showrooms. They have no idea what it's like in the front line or what problems we dealers face.'

'So you don't want to sell me a VanXL then?'

'Look, you're perfectly welcome to come to our showrooms and take a look at the VanXL here. If you like it, you can buy it. If you don't, then don't. It's as simple as that. The people that are always screaming to test-drive cars hardly ever buy them anyway, in my experience.'

'How much does the Van cost?' I ask, afraid that he's about to hang up on me.

'About 35,000 euros, depending what extras you want.' Should I be surprised that the only information the call centre could give me was wrong?

I don't have to put up with this, I think, and call the national marketing manager for AutoVan.

'We know we're having a few problems and, as you are perhaps aware, AutoVan has been struggling with a negative image for some time.' That was his answer.

'And, speaking as a potential customer, I can assure you that you have convinced me of that' was mine!

Amazingly good!

There is another way, as a car salesman in Austria proved. I expressed an interest in a family car in his showrooms. After giving me a friendly and brief run-down of the most important points, he handed me the keys and said: 'You won't know if it's the right car for you until you drive it.' We arranged that I would bring the car back in one hour. When I returned, I found my own car waiting for me, freshly washed. 'All part of the service,' he assured me.

A good friend was taking a short holiday in his sports car when, after only 80 kilometres, he noticed that there was something wrong. He took a room in a hotel, contacted the national office of the automobile company and described his problem to a mechanic. The mechanic made a note of the address and the registration number of the car, asked the customer to leave his keys at the hotel reception desk and said: 'I think you must be mistaken. Our cars don't break down.'

Angry because he still hadn't heard from the garage next morning, the customer phoned them again and complained. The mechanic said: 'Like I told you yesterday, our sports cars don't have that problem!' When my friend looked in the hotel garage, he found that his car had been repaired and also waxed and polished. The hotel management told him that two mechanics had driven over 100 kilometres to fix the problem overnight.

Another car dealer takes a digital photograph of every proud new owner of a car. Once he has familiarized his customers with all the details of their new car and handed it over to them, he also presents them with the picture, which has been framed in the meantime.

Recently, a colleague told me that he bought a car and, three hours later, received a text message with the following words: 'Dear Mr Amrein, we wish you a lot of fun with your new car and safe journeys! Your Soltermann Garage team.'

Another car dealer gives all customers who buy a car from

him a bouquet of flowers, which he places on the passenger seat when they collect their new car.

Unleaded, please!

'Unleaded' is not the terse comment of a filling station attendant in blue overalls who cleans the windscreen for me while the petrol is being pumped into my tank, but the one-word digital display on the petrol pump. Romanticism has given way to efficiency, even at the filling station.

For years now, I have been going to 'my' local filling station at least once a week, but I don't even know the manager's name, and he is not aware that I am one of his customers. He doesn't know why I fill up on petrol there and not elsewhere. Once I have inserted the appropriate piece of plastic in the slot, pressed 'Pump 2 – unleaded' and confirmed my choice, it takes me exactly two minutes to fill the tank. I wonder what exactly I do in those two minutes and start to do the sums in my head:

I do around 30,000 kilometres a year in my car, with a fuel consumption of about 3,000 litres of petrol, 'unleaded' and of unknown vintage. My tank holds 60 litres, which means I spend 50 times 2 minutes, 100 minutes, doing absolutely *nothing.*

I don't clean my windscreen with that worn and scruffy scraper in its bucket of indefinable liquid, nor do I check the tyre pressure. And I don't buy my groceries there, either, as 'my' filling station doesn't have a shop.

Amazingly good!

At a filling station, I once saw a young man with a canister of coffee on his back. He was pouring coffee from his own 'pump' into paper cups and serving it to customers in their cars.

In the shop that was part of another filling station, there was a basket of free fruit with a sign reading: Dear customers! Please help yourself to an apple! It comes from orchards in our beautiful South Tyrol and contains a wealth of important nutrients. Take one, with our thanks for visiting our region.

In a service station in France, I saw a group of students dressed as clowns performing in a small circus tent on an adjacent field. The local tourist office had come up with this idea to provide a little entertainment for children, to break the monotony on their long journey to their summer holiday destination.

One petrol station chain believes in catching its potential customers from the outset. On its website, learner drivers can find a free virtual driving instructor who will answer all their questions on driving. A clever way to attract and win customers, when you think of all the new driving licences that are issued each year.

Is the water temperature ok?

11.15–12.00, hairdressers, it says in my appointments diary, immediately followed by *12.15, Business lunch with Eliane Hager, journalist.* 'Is the water temperature ok?' asks the hairstylist as I screw my eyes up against the glare of the neon lighting. Every man (and probably every woman, too) hears this question at least three times on every visit to a hairdressing salon. And my answer is always the same: 'Yes, thanks. It's fine.' My answer is always the same because not once in the last 30 years has the water ever been too hot or too cold. Not at this hairdressing salon and not at any hairdressing salon anywhere in the world. When you come to think of it, in addition to being able to cut hair, a hairstylist should be able to select the right water temperature when washing a client's hair. So why ask?

Another not very customer-friendly feature of hairdressing salons is the range of magazines available. It is usually limited to the 'celebrity' press, and while such publications are certainly very popular, there must be many customers who would prefer something a little more demanding.

It's often said that hairdressers need the skills of a psychologist, as people often discuss personal matters with their hairstylist. Yet psychologists don't merely concern themselves with their patients on a superficial level. They deal with them as individuals, take notes, study their habits and propose ways to help them solve their problems. Whereas, although most people go back to the same salon again and again to get their hair cut, the service offered there often remains the same. Occasionally, someone will come up with an innovative idea and offer a discount for regular customers, but that's about it.

Amazingly good!

When the customers at one hairdressing salon make an appointment, they are informed how long it will take to have their hair done. The owner has noticed how stressed some people are when they arrive, as they have underestimated how long they will need.

A salon in Munich came up with a very clever idea. They confirm appointments via SMS on the same day when the booking is made, and even reserve a parking space for the customer!

A hairstylist in Frankfurt takes the service for his customers even further than that. While they are having their hair done, a salon employee will run errands for them, ranging from taking the dog for a walk to doing the grocery shopping.

And on the subject of stress: a salon in Lucerne offered me a free hand massage. As trainee hairdressers also learn how to give hand massages, this gives them extra training and is an added service to the customer.

After my fourth visit to his salon, one hairdresser realized that I was a satisfied customer and offered to phone me when it was time for another appointment. He had noticed that I often left it so late that they couldn't fit me in at such short notice.

Another hairdresser found out quite a lot about me while chatting as he cut my hair, for example which hair gel I use and what my hobbies are. The next time I came for a haircut, I found a mountain-bike magazine waiting for me. He also recommended a new and better hair gel, which, of course, I bought from him.

Another bright idea is that of a hairstylist who has found a way to combine his hobby with his profession. He has set up a little photographic studio in his salon and offers his customers professional-quality 'before and after' photos. Many customers jump at the chance to get new photographs taken. After all, when better to have portrait photos taken than when you've just had your hair done? The success of this idea proves him right!

In the United States, I visited a hairdressing salon where

customers could watch TV if they wanted. Ideal for those who would prefer not to chat with their stylist.

And in Sydney, I got the best haircut of my life! When I returned to the same salon two months later, the stylist welcomed me, but did not recognize me. When he looked at my hair in the mirror, however, he said confidently: 'That's my work, isn't it?' Quite amazed, I asked him how he could be so sure. He answered: 'Every haircut bears the signature of the hairdresser, and your haircut bears mine!'

The smallest room – a horror scenario

What do you do when you need a toilet and you are not at home? Of course you can dive into a hotel or a restaurant, but somehow that often makes me feel like a parasite. I'm afraid the head waiter is going to throw me out with the words: 'Our washrooms are only for our paying guests, sir!' In most places, they simply don't appreciate how problematic a full bladder can be.

So, if like me, you don't fancy trying to sneak into a hotel or restaurant unnoticed, your only alternative will be public conveniences. The first problem is that you can never find one when you need it, and then, if you have managed to find one, the chances are that it will be in a disgusting state. I always thank my lucky stars that I'm a man and try not to think what it must be like to be a woman and have to use a public toilet.

You think I'm making a fuss about nothing? There has been in-depth research into this subject, as the following data show. On average, women use the toilet five times a day, men only three times. Women, however, spend an average of 18 minutes every day in the toilet, men only 15 minutes. On each visit, men spend an average of 5 minutes, women only 3.6 minutes. If you take into consideration the fact that the average life expectancy for a woman is 82.5 years and for a man 76.5 years, you will see that a woman spends 376 days of her life in the toilet! And though the figure is not so high for men, it is still 291 days!

And many of these days are not spent in the privacy of our own bathrooms, but in other toilets, for example in hotels, restaurants, stations or airports. And though most people are familiar with the saying that the washrooms say a lot about a company, the message doesn't seem to have sunk in, and not only with the railway companies. I estimate that at least 50 per cent of public toilets are in a revolting state. The graffiti and the damage to the walls left behind by previous visitors are a telling reflection on the state of our society. I find it particularly surprising that no bright spark has seized the opportunity to beat the vandals to it and use the walls for advertising purposes. A study carried out by the University of Applied Science in Bielefeld showed that 72 per cent of the people interviewed would find advertising in public toilets a welcome diversion. And it is an established fact that 12 per cent of people read on the toilet.

The following examples illustrate that using a public toilet can indeed be a positive experience!

Amazingly good!

There are an increasing number of companies who specialize in running public toilets. For just 1 euro, you get a freshly cleaned toilet seat, can freshen up or even take a shower. There are baby's changing tables, and the toilets are taken care of by a friendly attendant in a clean uniform.

In one airport hotel, I found that the toilet doors were marked Economy Class, Business Class and First Class. Of course, I looked into all three toilets, and they all seemed identical... except for the toilet paper, which was single-layer in the Economy Class, double-layer in the Business Class and triple-layer in the First Class toilet. The guests found this witty idea quite amusing.

In a New York restaurant, I found a designer toilet with urinals built of TV screens behind a pane of glass. An impressive way for the man of the world to express his opinion of current TV programmes.

In another restaurant toilet, guests stand with their feet under a marble cover in front of the urinals. On this cover are the words 'Keep your shoes clean!' Male guests found this idea, too, very innovative.

An amusing anecdote: a travel agency in Southern Germany received a letter from a male customer complaining about the toilets in his hotel. The letter read: 'When I sat on the toilet, my genitals were immersed in the water.' The travel agency wrote back to the customer: 'We tried these toilets ourselves, but were unable to immerse our genitals in the water. Please contact the *Guinness Book of Records.*'

Children welcome

... it said on the menu board in front of the restaurant. Whenever I read anything like this, I wonder what the Human Rights Commission in The Hague would have to say about such signs. It seems obvious to me that all guests are welcome in a restaurant, irrespective of age and height.

I had two small guests with me. My son Noah was 18 months old and Christina, the daughter of friends of mine, was one week short of her third birthday. I had offered to take the two children for a meal in town so that the two mothers could enjoy an undisturbed shopping spree.

'Smoking or non-smoking?' the waiter asked me in a very professional tone, as I entered the restaurant flanked by the two children. The Americans' answer to that question would be: 'Having a smoking section in a restaurant is like having a peeing section in a pool!'

'Non-smoking,' I answer and am shown to a table for two while I try to stop Christina running off in the opposite direction and Noah grabbing food from other tables. Before I can ask, the waiter says: 'I'm sorry, but we only have three high chairs, and they are all in use at the moment.' Uh, huh, I think to myself. Children are welcome, but you don't provide kiddie-sized chairs for them. My son is such a live wire that only a high chair could save me from a very taxing trial of nerves, but the waiter has just robbed me of all my illusions.

I order a mixed salad, for Noah a very small portion of spaghetti with tomato sauce (his favourite). 'We have a children's menu,' the waiter proudly announces. But Noah doesn't want the Mickey Mouse Menu, just a small portion of spaghetti with tomato sauce. Christina is quite capable of ordering her own meal. At just three years of age, she has a vocabulary of 8,000 words, can read, and can decide for herself what she wants and what she doesn't want. Yet I have rarely found a restaurant where the staff hand the children the menu or take their orders directly. They usually only communicate with the children via their parents. Children notice this, however, and can be damning in their judgement.

'Careful! The plates are very hot!' someone says from behind me, and instinctively, I spread my arms out left and right to prevent Noah and Christina burning themselves. 'Sorry, but you can't seriously be going to serve two small children their meals on hot plates. Don't you have children's plates?' 'No,' the waiter answers in an exasperated tone, 'but I could tip it onto another plate.'

Something smells bad around here. It can't be the food; the first couple of bites were delicious. Just as I thought: the unpleasant odour is coming from Noah's nappy. While Christina tucks into her plate of Uncle-Dagobert's Treasure, I grab my son and dash off to the *Ladies*. Yes, you read right. The Ladies. You never find a changing table in the men's toilets. So I fix that apologetic, strained smile on my face again and walk through the door, to meet strained smiles from the women reflected in the make-up mirror. I say the make-up mirror because they don't even have changing tables in the Ladies here. As if I hadn't already noticed just how welcome the little ones are in this restaurant.

Not long after arriving back at my table, I ask for the bill, and when it comes, I see that they have charged the full price for Noah's tiny portion of spaghetti. Children's portions are only available from the children's menu. If you order anything else, you pay the full adult price.

Two small diners and one grown-up guest leave the restaurant, relieved. 'Well, did you three have a good time?' the two mums ask as they hug their offspring. My face must have spoken volumes, because they didn't wait for an answer.

Amazingly good!

The following examples show that there is a better way.

A hotel in an Austrian resort has a Children's Club with trained staff. The special service here is that, when they check in, parents are given a bleeper so that the babysitter can get in touch with them at any time. This way, they don't need to worry how their children are.

In another restaurant, the children's playground is right next to the garden patio, so parents can keep an eye on their children at all times.

At one very child-friendly restaurant, the chef collects children from the restaurant whenever he can and gives them a tour of the kitchens. At this restaurant, children can also sit and eat at their own colourful children's table, separate from their parents.

Pizza Quattro Cartone

Brrrinng! goes the doorbell. Exactly 35 minutes ago, I ordered a Pizza Quattro Stagione, a Pizza Margharita, two Insalata Caprese and two portions of tiramisu.

Some evenings, when we aren't in the mood to go out to a restaurant or are just too lazy to cook, I phone the pizza service 'around the corner'. I say around the corner because almost all home delivery services advertise how close they are to your home and how fast their delivery service is.

'Hello! Here is your order, sir,' says the young man in motorcycle leathers. 'That's 31 euros, please,' he adds. 'One pizza is free, because it's your tenth.' I suddenly remember that I have a regular customer card. 'Keep the change,' I say as I give him the money with one hand and try to balance the boxes and plastic dishes in the other.

The two cardboard boxes feel lukewarm, and when we open them, my girlfriend and I find that the contents are not necessarily hot just because it says 'Hot Pizza' on the box. But we are too hungry to bother with reheating them in the oven. We always split the pizzas in half and swap. Pizza is always difficult to cut, especially a take-away. The once crispy base of our two pizzas now has the consistency of a Swiss cheese fondue and refuses obstinately to be cut.

Once we have finished our gourmet Italian at-home meal, we look at each other and exchange views, just as we would if we had eaten at a restaurant. In this case, we are agreed: 'The pizza wasn't exactly a hit,' says my girlfriend. 'But the salad was ok, and the tiramisu was excellent,' I add. We both realize simultaneously that that's what we say every time we order a take-away pizza. I pour bitters into two liqueur glasses and hope that they will make the meal more digestible.

We learnt three things from this, namely:

1. that pizza is probably the least suitable meal for a take-away;

2. that we would be happier if every tenth pizza was not free, but as good as it tastes in the restaurant; and

3. that in future, we will go back to ordering sushi instead.

Amazingly good!

One company in Zurich has specialized in take-away meals and delivers meals from your favourite restaurant to your home.

A pizza delivery service brings you your pizza in special heated containers. Customers pay a small deposit for such a container. The next time they order a pizza, the messenger takes the old container back with him. This is the best system I have come across so far.

In the retirement home

On the one hand, I really enjoy visiting my grandmother in her retirement home, because she really means the world to me, but on the other, I hate the clinical atmosphere at 'Zur Linde', her retirement home. My grandmother knows this, but she always says: 'Leave it, dear. Everyone here is really quite nice.'

Believe me, I do appreciate the work done by the staff of such homes all over the world, and I am quite aware that, as a businessman, I would never be able to do this complex job myself. And I do hope that someone will take care of me when I reach my grandmother's age. In 53 years time, I will be as old as my grandmother is now, and I would like to use that time to draw attention to a few things that just don't make sense.

The clothes drawers in my grandmother's room are so low down that she has trouble bending to take out fresh garments. The TV set hangs on the wall in the corner of the room, which means that my grandmother can only watch TV by tilting her head back and craning her neck. Her 91-year-old neck.

The keypad on her telephone has keys of normal size. Imagine you are a 91-year-old lady with bad eyesight and trembling hands and try to dial your grandson or granddaughter's number. I'm betting you couldn't. More than once, she dialled a complete stranger's number, until I stored the most important numbers for her on speed-dialling keys. Still, the keys are too small and, in my opinion, it is the responsibility of the home to ensure that telephones with large keypads are installed in all the rooms. The same goes for the remote controls for TV and radio sets.

In general, the writing on all signs and labels in the home is too small, both in the rooms themselves and in the corridors. Neither the architect nor the person directly responsible for the signs was working with the customers' best interests at heart here, which is a pity. Making an elderly person's life easier is such a rewarding task.

But recently, when I offered to mention these things to the manager of the home, my grandmother just said again: 'Leave it dear. Everyone here is really quite nice.'

Amazingly good!

A retirement home on Lake Constance has completely embraced the cause of meeting the requirements of all its residents. The home has its own small zoo with pets and its own library in a conservatory built especially to house it.

The menu is in large print and the staff are familiar with the likes and dislikes of all the residents (favourite foods, favourite drink, favourite colour, favourite flowers, etc).

The staff also organize regular trips for the residents. They have even been to see an international football match together!

A trip to the mountains

We all need to escape the hustle and bustle of everyday life once in a while, to relax and get away from it all.

Unfortunately, when we arrived at the car park in front of the mountain railway station where we hoped to flee the world of business for the world of relaxation, we saw that thousands of others had had exactly the same idea. 'Drive down to the end of the car park, and someone will direct you to a parking space, sir,' a car park attendant dressed from head to foot in fluorescent colours calls to me through the window.

Once we enter the station building, things start to get hectic: 'You get the tickets and I'll see if I can get us something to drink,' my girlfriend says, and off she goes. And, left standing in the queue in front of the ticket window, I do what I always do in such situations: I study the people around me. In this case, I study the station employees. And as I watch them, a vague thought starts to form at the edge of my mind, but I can't quite grasp it.

'Yes?' says the woman behind the thick glass of the ticket window, bringing me firmly back to earth. 'Two return tickets,' I say, and two seconds later, the words '38 euros' appear in red lettering on a display, accompanied by 'That will be 38 euros, sir,' from the employee, her voice croaky through the microphone. My tickets and my change are delivered to me through a turntable device below the window.

I am reminded of scenes from various films I have seen where someone uses a telephone to speak to a prisoner separated from them by a thick pane of glass. If the two people are a couple in love, the scene ends with them each pressing a hand against the glass in an attempt to achieve some measure of more intimate contact.

I am very tempted to re-enact such a scene with the woman behind the ticket window, a Ms Haibling, but in view of the long queue of people behind me, all eager to get away from it all, I decide against it.

Suddenly I remember a newspaper article I read, in which a journalist bemoaned the *lack of the personal touch* in the tourism industry. And how right he was. Customer-orientation begins in the car park or at the ticket office.

'Tickets, please!' a voice calls, just as my attention is caught by something else that has always bothered me about the staff on such mountain railways: their stuffy uniforms! Instead of choosing a uniform which would reflect the corporate identity, they always clothe their employees in different shades of blue, according to the motto: blue is always good! It's not that the uniforms they choose are bad; the question is simply whether a different uniform wouldn't be more appropriate and therefore better!

And when the 'Chief Ticket Inspector' has inspected both us and our tickets with military precision and moved on, my girl-friend whispers in my ear: 'It wouldn't hurt him to smile.' Before I can answer, a voice booms through the loudspeakers: 'Ladies and gentlemen, welcome to one of Europe's most popular mountain railways. In his day, Mark Twain compared our mountain with...'. They can't ask Mark Twain for his opinion any more. But they could ask us instead!

Amazingly good!

I particularly remember one mountain railway in Switzerland that clothes its staff in a trendy Swiss ethno look. These local guides were more than happy to provide tourists with information on the region and helped passengers on and off the trains rather than restricting themselves to inspecting tickets.

In one cable car in Switzerland, the cable car attendant read aloud the menu for the day from the restaurant on the top of the mountain – in the languages of all the passengers in the car.

In one cable car I once travelled on in Bavaria, the cable car attendants yodelled on the way up the mountain!

At the supermarket

'Dear customers, today our master butcher recommends our prime quality calf's liver, one hundred grams for just 1 euro 85 cents . And, for the whole of August, we have a special offer on our bumper pack of sanitary towels.' Not that voice again, I think as I steer my oversized trolley determinedly on the shortest route to the soft drinks section.

Wherever you may be in the world, when you enter a super-market you are always welcomed by the same glib, over-friendly and artificially cheerful loudspeaker announcements. Not only is the message always identical; I am firmly convinced that it's always the same person reading it. Just imagine all the 'Dear customers' storming the checkouts, their trolleys piled high with calf's liver and bumper packs of sanitary towels!

My trolley laden with orange juice, spring water and a few other items that weren't on my shopping list, I turn the corner from the cereal aisle into the pasta aisle, and all at once I make eye contact with a friendly, smiling woman. She is almost concealed behind a tower of artfully presented cubes of cheese on cocktail sticks. Instinctively, I wonder how I can avoid the inevitable sales patter. 'Would you like to try some, sir?' She smiles and holds out a cube of cheese on a little silver platter with a paper napkin. 'No thanks, I'm not hungry!' I say, pointing to my stomach to underline my idiotic reply. Idiotic because you don't have to be hungry to eat a 1-centimetre cube of cheese and because I have now outed myself as a particularly dim-witted customer. And that bothers me.

I arrive at the checkout. My purchases are scanned and, after the obligatory 'peep', are transported to the back of the desk for packing. 'No, I don't have a customer card.' 'No, I don't collect the discount stamps,' I reply to the stereotypical questions. 'Thirty-six thirty change, sir.'

'Hello,' the woman on the checkout says to the customer behind me, who has separated his purchases from mine with one of those little plastic bars. The words 'Emmental, mild – Special offer double-pack' catch my eye as the customer on the next checkout places his purchases on the conveyor belt. Aha! A victim of the 'Cheese-Cubes-on-a-Silver-Platter Campaign'! Feeling a little proud of myself, I hold my head high, happy in the knowledge that I didn't fall for it!

Amazingly good!

A supermarket in the United States provides magnifying glasses for its older customers and customers with poor eyesight. These glasses enable them to read the information on the packages or on the shelves without having to ask for help.

A chain of fashion stores in the United States has found a very special way to attract more regular customers. On a series of designated days, customers can hand in worn clothing there. In return, they receive a $10 voucher valid on clothing purchases worth at least $50. The store gives the second-hand clothing to a charity organization.

A department store in the UK aims to persuade its customers to use the stairs instead of taking the escalator. Signs on all the escalators encourage shoppers to do something to improve their personal fitness. Normally, at most 10 out of 100 customers will take the stairs if there is an escalator. When these encouraging signs were introduced, that figure doubled. This rewarding yet simple marketing campaign also attracted a lot of media attention for the store.

In the United States, there is a special department store for outdoor freaks where customers spend an average of two to three hours per visit. The store has become a real tourist attraction and a meeting point for fans of leisure and outdoor activities. It has a waterfall, campfire sites located in the centre of an area with rock gardens, cycle and hiking trails, rain-testing chambers, refrigerated chambers for testing polar expedition equipment, light-testing rooms and a mountain peak for climbing, all with the aim not so much of presenting its products, but of giving its customers a taste of nature and the fun activities offered by the great outdoors.

A set of snow tyres, please

It's early November. It's warm outside, and somehow it's hard to imagine that winter is not far away. But the set of snow tyres stacked up in my cellar are an omnipresent reminder of the cold season. They lie next to the garden barbecue, a symbol of the summer. You get your hands dirty when you handle either of them, and they both need to be cleared away and stored ready for the appropriate season.

My summer tyres are rather worn, so I am forced to

exchange them for the winter ones early this year. I hate changing the tyres. It's such a long and laborious procedure:

1. I have to clear out the boot of my car and line it with plastic sheeting.

2. I lug the snow tyres up from the cellar, somehow always managing to get my clothes dirty in the process.

3. I pile the tyres alarmingly high into my boot, which is hardly big enough to accommodate them.

4. I drive to my tyre dealer, where I have made an appointment for 8.30 this morning. (Of course, this means that I have had to postpone a business appointment and explain to my boss.)

In the garage, it's as loud and hectic as when Michael Schumacher is making a pit stop, the only difference being that they don't work that fast here. I stand in front of a glass-fronted cubicle that serves as the office and wait for someone to notice me. I feel extremely overdressed in my business suit. Five minutes pass, and I'm starting to get nervous. I have a business appointment at 9.30, and I can't afford to miss it. The garage staff have obviously made an effort to help their male customers pass the time while they wait and have hung the Pirelli Calendars for 1994 to 2003 on the wall. I just wonder how women feel when they are expected to wait in front of a wall covered with 10 naked models draped languidly across car tyres.

'Are you Joe Friedmann?' asks a tall man in dirty overalls who has appeared in front of me. Before I can answer, he points me to a place on the platform.

Srrr, srrr, srrrr..., the electrically powered torque wrench buzzes efficiently, and just 18 minutes later, the same man appears again and presents me with the bill, leaving four dirty fingerprints on my hand. 'Your summer tyres will need replacing next spring. They're worn right down.'

At 10 o'clock that evening, I carry the four summer tyres down into the cellar and deposit them next to the barbecue. I study the bill and read the heading: '*Fast – efficient – economical*'. Below this, I find the sum, and then, right at the bottom, I am astounded to read the words: '*Storage service! Purchase your new tyres from us and we will store your summer/winter tyres for just 5 euros per tyre. Inquire at your garage!*'

Well, it seems I only had to ask.

Amazingly good!

One particularly astute tyre dealer offers three astounding services as standard:

1. Every time you change your tyres, you get your car windows and the rear-view mirror cleaned.

2. The garage places a refreshing tissue in the glove compartment of each car.

3. When the tyres have been changed, the garage always turns the car and parks it so that it can be driven straight off.

Another garage has introduced a clever discount system to avoid the rush when the first snow falls. Customers who have their winter tyres put on in October/November get an early bird discount. The garage starts phoning regular customers straight after the summer holidays to arrange appointments.

When I went to fill up the water for the windscreen wipers, I discovered that the garage had already done it for me and left a note saying: '*With us, you get good road holding... and good vision!*'

'*At our garage, sparkling clean tyres and wheel rims are all part of the service*' the brochure of a tyre dealer in Italy announces. They are true to their word and even put the tyres and wheel rims in handy bags with carrying handles. Their customers never have to worry about dirty car boots or getting their clothes soiled with brake dust.

One company in Germany offers a particularly comprehensive service. It has set up an interactive internet site where customers can ask a virtual expert questions. The home page features the latest tyre tests and information on where to get the best prices. Customers can even make an appointment to have their tyres changed at their nearest dealer.

We hope you have enjoyed flying with us

'Flight LJ is now ready for boarding,' the smartly dressed female airline employee croaks into the microphone. You can tell who is not a frequent flyer; they are the ones who all immediately jump up. Those who fly regularly remain calmly in their seats and carry on reading their newspapers. After all, they are flying Business Class, or even First Class. Nowhere will you find clearer evidence of a two-class society than when you fly. For some, flying is an exciting experience, for others tedious routine.

I am one of the latter group, a frequent flyer, and I can tell you that it really is no picnic. The only unpredictable element of a flight is whether you will ever actually reach your destination. Everything else is utterly and boringly predictable. Every part of the procedure and every announcement made by the captain is the same all over the world. Sometimes, I couldn't even say which airline I am flying with; they all look the same.

'Ladies and gentlemen, welcome on board our Flight LJ to Miami. We will be taking off in just a few minutes. Our estimated flight time is approximately…'. There's no need to hear the rest, we've all heard it so many times before. Why, I ask myself, doesn't an AUA captain greet his passengers with the traditional Austrian '*Grüß Gott*' and a Swissair captain with '*Grüezi*'? Why don't the airlines make more of the typical differences between countries?

For example:

Our flight to Miami will take 8 hours and 15 minutes. After going through Immigration, you can take a taxi to your hotel, where you can go for a swim in the sea, which has a temperature of 24 degrees Centigrade. The sun is shining and it is 28 degrees Centigrade in the shade. To get you in the mood, we will now be showing a Hollywood movie that was filmed in Miami. Relax and enjoy your flight, the food and the friendly service.

But no, on more than 200 flights, I have never heard anything like this. It would be nice to have a change, wouldn't it? But instead of individualized announcements that really grab your attention, we get the same standard, hackneyed phrases every time. And instead of a dish typical of the country we are flying to, we get turkey breast with rice and broccoli yet again.

'Our cabin staff will now demonstrate the safety procedures.' It amazes me that in so many years, no one has come up with a way to solve this serious problem. Rarely will more than 20 per cent of the passengers actively watch while the flight attendants rattle off this important information as though they are desperate to go to the toilet. And if the teachers won't learn, neither will the students.

The man in seat 7a has taken refuge behind his business broadsheet while the cabin staff go through the motions of demonstrating the safety procedures. He has probably seen and heard it all umpteen times before. I wonder what would happen if the stewardess handed him a lifejacket and said: 'You look like someone who has flown a lot, sir. Why don't you demonstrate the use of a lifejacket for us?' Wow, that would really make everyone sit up and take notice! He probably wouldn't be able to remember how to do it, but at least it would be an experience he wouldn't forget in a hurry.

It's like with a fire extinguisher: you won't learn how to use it by looking at it. Nevertheless, I can't see the service offered by the world's airlines changing at any time in the foreseeable future. It will most likely remain the same as ever: predictable, correct, but infinitely boring. 'We hope you have enjoyed flying with us,' the captain says.

Nothing against hoping, but knowing would be better.

Amazingly good!

In the 1980s, one US airline had its captains introduce every safety demonstration with the following announcement: 'Ladies and gentlemen, there are 50 ways to leave your lover, but only six exits from this airplane. With this in mind, please pay close attention to the following safety demonstration.'

Here's another example from the United States. One airline there had the clever idea of playing songs on the subject of flying in their in-flight programme. These songs included:

'In the Air Tonight' by Phil Collins

'Love is in the Air' by John Paul Young

'Flying' by the Beatles

'The Airport Song' by the Byrds

'Off the Ground' by Paul McCartney

'Walking in the Air' by Howard Blake

'Spread your Wings' by Queen, and many more.

At one airport in Canada, passengers can listen to information about the city while they are waiting for their suitcases at the Luggage Claim.

An overdose of perfume

One rainy Sunday afternoon, I was doing my crossword puzzle when one of the clues gave me the idea of going to a perfumery. The clue read '10 Across, Animal with an unpleasant smell (5)'. My train of thought is sometimes as difficult for others to follow as the clues to a crossword puzzle.

As that may be, next day finds me at the door to a perfumery. *'Come in and find out'* the poster on the window says. I push open the door and am immediately enveloped in a cloud of sweet, heavy perfume. I have hardly gone three steps when I am welcomed by two sales assistants dressed in what look like nurses' uniforms and escorted up the two steps into the sales area. 'How can I help you?' one of the two ladies asks me, giving the other a look that clearly signifies 'My customer.' 'I'm looking for a new perfume – or rather, a new aftershave,' I tell the lady in white. She reminds me of Snow White with her immaculate make-up, her scarlet lips and her black hair combed severely back.

'Are you looking for something specific?' asks Snow White, and draws me with her to a set of shelves stretching to the ceiling, at least two metres wide and full of shiny bottles and expensive-looking boxes.

'Not really,' I answer, and Snow White rattles of a list of possibilities that makes my head reel: 'Would you prefer something tangy and spicy or something sweeter, with flowery overtones – something fresh or lingering, something with a headier note or something sweeter and subtler, more lively?' 'Umm – I'm just looking for something masculine, something classic and neutral,' I state firmly. Snow White's cheeks start to heat up.

'Then I would recommend this one.' With a theatrical gesture, she sprays aftershave on a white goose quill and holds it directly under my nose. The strong smell of alcohol makes my nostrils twitch. I put on the look I use to impress wine waiters, the connoisseur look. 'Or this one,' she says, spraying another quill with another scent. And she keeps on spraying feather after feather with aftershave and waving it under my nose until I can't take it any more. Stop! The membranes in my nose feel swollen, and I've smelt so many aftershaves I can't remember which one I liked best. What I need now is a deep breath of fresh, clear and perfume-free air, and so I flee the perfumery – without my new aftershave! Of course, on my way out, Snow White presses a few trial samples in little glass phials into my hand.

I remember the poster on the window, '*Come in and find out*' – they couldn't have been more wrong. 'Come in and run out' is more like it. I hear the familiar ding-dong as the door opens, releasing me at last. I take a deep breath – the air is filled with the wonderful smell of fresh-baked rolls. 'Time for elevenses!' I think and turn my steps towards the bakery next door.

Amazingly good!

A well-known perfumery in a popular shopping mall has a special room with optimum ventilation. Customers are handed labelled, perfumed cards by the staff and take them to this room, where they can sniff them at their leisure while enjoying light refreshments.

A perfumery in Germany gave all its best customers a copy of the book *Perfume* by Patrick Süskind as a Christmas gift.

Cool Caribbean dream

A dull and chilly November day is drawing to a close, and I know that just a few rays of warm sunshine would do wonders to brighten my mood. However, the meteorologists are predicting more of the same grey, foggy weather over the next couple of days, so after work, I steer my car in the direction of the 'Caribbean Sun', my local tanning salon. Here, I hope to grab a few minutes of warming and heartening sunshine – even if it is artificial.

A bronzed beauty in a skimpy bikini smiles at me from the glossy poster where she leans against a palm tree. The slogan on the poster reads, '*A healthy suntan adds the finishing touches to any outfit*', and in the bottom right-hand corner, I read the name of the manufacturer of the solarium equipment. I take out my wallet and approach the metal change machine. I would much rather get my change from a friendly, smiling member of the solarium staff, but it's self-service here.

Blast! All I've got in my wallet is a 20-euro note, which means that as I had planned to buy 16 minutes of tanning time, I'm going to have 11 spare coins stretching my small wallet to its limits and bulging in the back pocket of my trousers!

My sunbed is occupied at the moment, so I sit down on an uncomfortable bistro chair and pick up the Caribbean's brochures on healthy tanning. I can hear the typical noise of the automatic lid opener and the humming of the fan intended to extract the thick, hot air from the room. A few minutes later, a boiled lobster comes out of the cubicle. His hair has seen better days and his scalp shines bright pink through his thinning locks. 'Piglet,' I think, as I notice the dried droplets of sweat on the plexiglas screen. With disinfectant, I remove all traces of my predecessor from the 'poolside lounger'. Barefoot, I walk backwards and forwards across the linoleum flooring, insert my coins in the slot of the machine and stretch my lily-white body out on the sun bed, which begins to groan and creak under my weight.

There is a clicking sound, and the fluorescent tubes above and below me start to glow brightly. Instead of something more suitable like 'Welcome to the Hotel California', I hear a mournful ballad by a German *Liedermacher* from the loudspeakers behind my head. Far from lightening my mood, this song with its romantic, mournful text always brings me down. It's getting hot sandwiched in the sunlounger, and the skin on my face is starting to feel tight. Sweat pools beneath my shoulder blades. My elbows hurt and the tight rubber of the protective goggles presses painfully against my eyeballs. Joe Friedmann – what on earth are you doing here?

Pling! The lights go out and the lid raises automatically – I'm free at last, and I stand up to admire my bronzed body in the mirror. With my tinted glasses, I look like an oversized housefly, and even without them, I can't see any difference in my appearance. Caribbean Sun – yeah, good joke!

What does this little solarium have in common with the Caribbean? *Nothing – nichts – nada – niente!*

At home, I take a shower. There's nothing worse than the smell of your skin after a visit to the solarium. I look at my back in the mirror and see the two white patches on my shoulder blades and the big, oval white patch on my backside. When I turn around, I see the egg-sized pale patches around my eyes. I suddenly realize that I look like a spectacled bear from the front – and a giant panda from the back!

Amazingly good!

In Munich, I discovered a solarium that really does conjure up a little Caribbean flair. There is a refreshments bar there, and every sun bed is equipped with a CD player. Customers can either choose one of the wide range of CDs available or even bring their own favourite CD from home.

I made another interesting discovery in the United States. I found a solarium with real sand and beautiful pictures of exotic beaches from all over the world. For visitors with children, there is even a cubicle with a play corner including sand moulds, etc.

Wanted – fashion consultant

Even though I am a businessman who spends a lot of his time travelling, I do occasionally find the time to stroll through the menswear department of one of the big clothing stores. Today, it's leisurewear I'm looking for – I get enough of suits and ties at work!

Though the marketing experts definitely wouldn't put me in the category 'Young Men', that's the department I make for, hoping they won't give me weird looks. Hip-hop is booming from the oversized loudspeakers mounted next to a poster showing a young, good-looking man. This male model with his perfect six-pack is having his jeans done up by a woman standing behind him. She is reaching around from the back and helping him fasten (or unfasten?) his trousers.

'Twelve thirty-eight to 14, please; twelve thirty-eight to 14, please,' a shrill voice calls much too loudly from the loud-speakers, a brief respite from the racket they were broadcasting before. I wonder who introduced that idiotic numbering system. Most people are given a complete name shortly after birth, and here they turn them into numbers.

I'm standing helplessly in front of a floor-to-ceiling shelving element, wondering as usual what size my bottom half is. Is it 34/38 or 36/38? I take one pair of trousers after another from the shelf and hold them up against me. Straight away, I reject three of the pairs I pick up. I think I have definitely outgrown the torn and patched jeans phase. I look desperately for a sales assistant to help me in my moment of need. 'Twelve thirty-eight to Joe Friedmann, please. Twelve thirty-eight to Joe Friedmann – help! Where are you?'

I grab three pairs of jeans in different sizes and colours and look for the changing rooms. The cubicles here are of the 'Western Saloon' type and have those swinging doors that cover only the middle part of you (and more or less of that, depending on how tall you are), and they remind me of old John Wayne movies. To prevent embarrassing encounters, I walk up and down the row of cubicles, bent at the waist, looking for one without bare feet showing under the door. I find a free cubicle, and, cool as John Wayne in his prime, I give the doors a hefty push – only to have them slam loudly into the walls on either side of the cubicle. The first pair of jeans I try on is a no-go – far too short and only suitable for wading in rock-pools. The second pair is the right length, but unfortunately, I can't do them up. The oversized white plastic anti-theft device has been mounted right on the button placket. My third and last attempt fails, too. I pull up the zip, only to have the metal tag come off in my hand.

I decide to go for option four, which is to stick with that faithful pair of jeans waiting for me at home and which has served me so well for so many years.

On my way to the escalator, I pass the poster of the male model with his six-pack and the beautiful girl again. What a lucky man, I think. He's wearing a pair of jeans that fit him like a glove, and he's even got his own fashion consultant and maid to help him dress.

Amazingly good!

In a fashion store in a large city, customers can go to the information desk and inform staff there what they are looking for. The staff then page trained personnel from the corresponding department and someone will come and accompany the customer to the relevant department.

One Swiss company offers its customers support with the help of computers. Customers are photographed in their underwear, the computer measures their proportions automatically from the photograph and calculates the correct size needed – in everything from socks or stockings to bras. The computer also suggests designers and brands suited to the customer's type. Then customers can buy all their clothes without problems via the internet and don't have to worry that the garments they order won't fit.

Another fashion store has fitted sensors to the doors of the changing cubicles so that customers can see if they are vacant or not. And the doors are solid fixed doors with a gap of only 10 centimetres at the top and bottom.

A tie dealer in Starnberg already does half his business via the internet, a fact that is at least partly due to the intriguing and handy online service he offers. A virtual model tries on the tie the customer selects with a variety of suits and shirts in different colours. This way, the customer can see straight away whether the tie he likes will go with the suit he has hanging in his wardrobe.

A menswear store in London guarantees to make any minor alterations required, for example, letting trousers out at the waistband, immediately, so that customers don't have the bother of returning to the store to pick up their suits or having them delivered.

Can I help you?

This is the most common way of greeting customers in clothing stores. 'Thank you, I'm just looking,' is the most common answer. At least, that's what most men answer, and we often look as though we could do with a little help in clothing stores.

Why do we go through this question-and-answer ritual then? Let us analyse the situation. On one hand we have a sales assistant whose prime objective, apart from helping the customer, is to sell something. On the other hand we have a customer who would like to look around, but above all to buy something.

Wouldn't it be much easier if the sales assistant said: 'Good afternoon, sir. What would you like to buy?' As a customer, I would then answer: 'I need a suit. For autumn. With a tie. And I want some Burlington socks and Calvin Klein underwear.' The sales assistant would then know exactly what my type is and could offer me professional advice. And in turn, I would get to buy all the things I need without having to slink around the store with a guilty conscience, only to be forced to admit in the end that I do need help after all!

I am standing in front of the menswear store where I have shopped regularly for years. Every year, on my birthday, they send me a personalized card informing me that I am entitled to 10 per cent discount on purchases made in the next three weeks. And by coincidence, today is my birthday! I enter the store with the idea of treating myself to a little birthday present at 10 per cent discount.

'Can I help you, sir?' an attractive and friendly female sales assistant asks.

'Yes, indeed,' I smile back. 'It's my birthday today, and I thought I would take advantage of your 10 per cent discount!'

'What 10 per cent discount, sir?' the sales assistant asks incredulously.

'Every year, this store sends me a birthday card with a voucher entitling me to 10 per cent discount on all purchases made within the following three weeks.'

'May I see the voucher, sir?'

'I'm sorry, I left it at home, but I'm sure you could check on your computer,' I suggest. After all, computers always know everything, I think to myself.

'One moment, please,' the sales assistant says and disappears behind a partition, where she enters into a heated discussion with the manageress. I overhear the tail end of the conversation '… tell him to come back with the voucher.'

'Er, I'm very sorry, sir,' the sales assistant tells me, obviously embarrassed because she knows I overheard the conversation, 'but this campaign is coordinated by the marketing department in our central office. I'm afraid I can't give you the discount without the voucher.'

I can't believe my ears. A typical case of the left hand not knowing what the right hand is doing. And so I try my luck with a trick.

'That's a pity,' I say. 'Can I at least give you my new address for your files, then?'

'Certainly, sir,' she answers and clicks to open the customer files. 'Your name, please?' 'Joe Friedmann.'

She enters 'Friedmann' and can't find me in the files. This is hardly surprising. For years they have been sending me letters addressed to 'Mr Fridmann' because someone was too lazy to read my credit card details properly.

'Try looking under "Fridmann".'

'Yes, here it is,' she says, obviously relieved. 'What is your new address?' she asks, without making any effort to correct the spelling of my name.

As I now have a clear view of the screen, I ask: 'Notice anything?' 'Sorry, sir?' she asks, clearly confused.

'My date of birth!' 'What about it, sir?'

'It's my birthday today!' I reply and simply can't believe that even now, she shows no reaction. She should surely have the courtesy to wish me a happy birthday. And surely she should now say: 'Of course you can take advantage of our special birthday discount, sir. After all, it is your birthday!'

But nothing of the kind happens. For one brief moment, I consider getting angry, but then I think better of it. After all, I am the customer. Let their marketing department keep sending their birthday cards to Mr Fridmann. Let them go on investing their marketing budget in me. I will certainly be shopping elsewhere from now on.

Amazingly good!

When shopping for a new suit in a menswear store recently, I couldn't remember my size. Instead of reaching for her tape measure, the sales assistant asked me if I had shopped there before. When I said I had, she went away to check on the computer, came back and said: 'Well, Mr Friedmann, I see you bought a blue suit from us last autumn. Does it still fit you?' 'Perfectly' I answered.

'Then this ought to be the right size,' she said, picking out a suit and accompanying me to the changing rooms.

When I had paid for the suit at the till, she handed me a

laminated card the size of a business card, with the words: 'To make it easier for you in future, I've made a note of your individual shirt, trouser and jacket size.'

Please hold the line

My last mobile phone bill was alarmingly high, so I decided to ask my provider to send me a so-called itemized bill. Quite a simple request – at least that's what I thought until I dialled the freefone number. I was just about to state my name and the purpose of my call when I realized that the friendly voice on the other end of the line was a recorded message. 'Hello, Yellow Sunstar here. If you would like to select a different language, please press 1. If you would like to learn more about our current special offers, please press 2. If you would like to register as a new customer, please press 3. If you have an inquiry concerning your bill, please press 4. If you would like to learn more about our services, please press 5.'

I now know what options I have, but I can't remember what key to press for what, so there's nothing for it. I have to dial 0800 all over again. 'Hello, Yellow Sunstar here. If you would like…' and so on and so forth. This time, I make a mental note of the key I need – number 4 – press it expectantly and *toottoot-toottoot* – I have been disconnected. Would you believe it? But I'm not about to give in that easily.

I dial 0800. 'Hello, Yellow Sunstar here. If you…'. I press 4 immediately so I don't have hear the whole spiel again, and hey presto, a click tells me that this time, I am being put through. The phone rings twice, and then a recording of the song 'Time to say goodbye' in an instrumental version starts to play. This emotional and melancholy interlude is interrupted by a recorded voice saying, 'Please hold the line.' The first melody is followed by 'Strangers in the night', and then, at last, someone on the other end picks up the phone. 'Yellow Sunstar, good morning. My name is Susanne Eisner. How may I help you?'

Yippee! Number 4 lives! I think to myself, and inform Ms Eisner that I would like an itemized bill. 'I'm sorry,' she says, 'I'll have to put you through to a colleague.' I just have time to recognize the last few bars of 'Strangers in the night', then a voice on the other end of the line says, 'Yellow Sunstar. Good morning. My name is Lars Johannson. How may I help you?' Once again, I briefly state my request. 'Is the mobile phone registered to you personally or to your company, sir?' the man with the cool voice from the far north of Europe inquires. 'It's a company phone.' 'Then I'm afraid I'm going to have to hand you over to a colleague. Company accounts are handled by a different department – one moment, please.'

I can't believe my ears. This time, however, there is no musical interlude, and another voice answers immediately: 'Yellow Sunstar. Good morning. My name is Jutta Kleinschmid. How may I help you?' Exactly the same wording yet again. They certainly believe in quality management at Yellow Sunstar – or has an industry standard been created for telephone calls?

I pull myself together and, for the third time, explain that all I want is a teensy-weensy itemized bill. By this time, I am seething inside and have trouble stopping my voice trembling with anger. 'What's the postal code for your company's address?' Ms Kleinschmid asks. I answer '66045' meekly, and Jutta labours away at her keyboard. 'Mr Friedmann? Ms Müller is the person to handle your request. Your company is in her area,' she says and asks me to wait a moment. Unfortunately, my patience is running out by now. I am scribbling nervously with my pencil on my notepad. I have already noted four different names on it, and all the smileys I doodled while listening to 'Time to say goodbye' have now got horns and the corners of their mouths are firmly turned down.

'Yellow Sunstar. Good morning. My name is Daniela Müller. How may I help you?' 'You can save my life by preventing me having a heart attack!' I answer. I hear a surprised 'Sorry?' 'It's ok,' I say, state the name of my company and my simple request for that little list of calls made, in the hope of hearing, at long last, the words: 'Certainly, sir!' And the miracle actually happens! After almost a quarter of an hour spent being passed from one department to another, I can finally expect to receive an itemized bill by mail within the next 10 days – for a charge of 10 euros. 'Time to say goodbye,' I tell Frau Müller, who reacts with a startled 'Pardon me?' 'Nothing,' I reply, put down the phone and collapse onto my office chair.

Amazingly good!

Only once has a call centre employee managed to impress me, and she was working for a bank. Right at the beginning of our conversation, she told me: 'I will be your contact person from now on. Later today, you will receive an e-mail from me with my name, my extension number and details of times when I can be reached, so that you can contact me more easily. The list also includes the name and number of the person who takes over from me when I go on holiday.'

Open wide!

I can definitely think of a thousand more pleasant ways to
spend my time than at the dentist's. But like it or not, I can't
put it off any longer, as one of my molars has been reminding
me ever since Sunday morning when I bit into my wholegrain
breakfast roll and a filling fell out. And so here I am in the
waiting room, palms moist with sweat. I swear I'll never eat a
wholegrain roll again. Idly, I turn the worn and sweat-marked
pages of a more or less well-known glossy women's magazine.
Just as I am trying my best to immerse myself in one of its
riveting and very profound articles, the loudspeaker over the
door booms out: 'Mr Friedmann to Examination Room 2,
please.'

Taking one more deep breath, I dry my hands on the legs of
my trousers and take my place on the 'electric chair'. A Ms
Bettina Christ fastens a bib around my neck and tells me the
dentist will be with me in just a moment. To my left, a pink
tablet fizzes in its glass, and the blinding light of the lamp
above me hurts my eyes. There I sit, awaiting my fate. I close my
eyes and try to imagine that the fizzing sound and the glaring
light are really the surf and sun of a Pacific island.

I am rudely awakened from my dream by a voice saying:
'Good afternoon Mr Friedmann.' The dentist asks how I am
and extends a disinfected hand. I offer him my sweaty palm.
'Open wide!' I hear him mumble from behind his mask, and
before I know it, his horrible-tasting silicon gloves, complete
with fingers, mirror and a poker-like instrument, are probing
around in my mouth. And that's only the start of it – he clamps
three pads of a size 'for those heavier days' inside my upper
and lower lip. I feel like Marlon Brando in *The Godfather*.

Out comes the drill and he sets to work on my damaged molar.

'What happened?' he asks, while Bettina expertly wields the saliva extractor. 'Ahh haaa aa ahhaaha aa aha ahhaahhaah- haaahaa ahhha,' I answer in a valiant attempt to explain my mishap with the bread roll, though try as I might, there's no way I can utter a single coherent word with all that stuff in my mouth.

'Are you ok?' he asks. 'Ah aahh ahaha ahhh,' I gurgle, wondering whether he can understand a word of what I'm saying. There's only one logical explanation for the fact that he always asks me questions while I am absolutely incapable of uttering anything but these pathetic mumbles. Trying to decipher the babblings of their helpless patients must be some peculiar form of job enrichment or a favourite hobby for dentists. But at least when it's all over I get the chance to prove that I am in fact capable of civilized conversation as I take my leave. I get out of that chamber of torture as fast as I can!

On my way home, I realize that it's not really over yet. I know I'm going to get that sinking feeling in my stomach again when the bill arrives. Dentists' bills are incomprehensible, written in some secret code, and as a mere patient, you have no hope of deciphering them:

No.	Pos.	Ser.	Tax
1	4001	Loc. anaes. Mefenacid	11.0

Amazingly good!

One dentist treats his surgical gloves with a pleasant-tasting mouth spray. This is much more agreeable than the taste of rubber in your mouth. He also takes the time to speak at length to his patients before commencing with the treatment, asking and answering questions.

Patients consulting another dentist near Bonn often recommend him to friends and family as he is very good with children. On their first visit to his surgery, he asks them with that typical stern dentist's expression on his face: 'Well, do you clean your teeth regularly?' The children, of course, always answer: 'Yes!' In the same strict tone, the dentist says: 'Well, I think we'll just check whether you really do.' Then he grins and beckons the child to the dentist's chair. And what happens then? He lets the children brush *his* teeth for him! While they are doing so, he takes the opportunity to praise them and to offer tips. The whole procedure is great fun for all involved, and at the end of it, his little patients get comic children's toothbrushes.

Another dentist has screens mounted on the ceiling above the chair so his patients can watch selected short films if they like.

Take a seat in the waiting room

A survey found that most executives, if asked what their weak points are, would answer 'I'm not very patient.' Sitting in my doctor's waiting room, I suddenly remember that survey.

At least I'm not alone. There are two other patients waiting with me, and we are all in collective waiting mode. Each one of us is reading one of the range of long-outdated magazines arranged in neat piles according to title on a table. Directly in front of me, I have three magazines to choose from: a general interest publication with a picture of President Bush preparing to wage war on Iraq, *Animal World*, with a miniature pony in full gallop on the cover, and *Gala*, which announces the thrilling news that Boris Becker and his wife have split up. In the corner, there are a few sad-looking toys. The walls are decorated with landscape prints: Oak Tree in the Mist, Waterfall with Rainbow, Snow-Capped Mountain Peak and... a representation of Christ complete with a dried palm leaf. Behind me, there is a series of diplomas all attesting to the great professional expertise of my GP. The only problem is, I can't understand half the medical terms on them.

What exactly is going wrong here, I wonder? Why doesn't my doctor see that here is an opportunity to change a predictably boring and depressing situation and make it a different and more interesting experience? His customers (I deliberately refrain from calling them patients) are penned up in a room and don't know how to occupy themselves. No one speaks, and the mood is subdued. We're like sinners waiting for the Last Judgement. Surely even a little music would help to lighten the atmosphere. A little background noise would break the silence and encourage people to chat.

The door opens and the receptionist inquires: 'Mrs Ettlin?' The elderly lady next to me reaches for her crutches, heaves herself to her feet, breathing heavily, and walks to the door, while the receptionist gives us a stiff little smile as if to say, 'This is going to take just a little bit longer.'

I look at my watch and wonder what the difference between

a moment and an eternity is. 'Waiting room.' I try to find other, more fitting names for it. For example, 'Room for eternity' or, 'The most boring room in the world' or even, 'No-talking room'!

A mother comes in with her roughly 3-year-old son, sits down and begins to answer his constant barrage of questions in a low whisper. 'Mummy, why aren't the man and the lady talking?' 'Because you don't talk in a waiting room,' his mother whispers back. I can't hold my tongue any longer: 'It's called a waiting room and not a silent room. And it's not called a whispering room, either, so why are we whispering?' The woman looks surprised at my rhetorical attack. She's obviously embarrassed and afraid that I am undermining her authority. 'That's just the way it is. A waiting room isn't a discotheque,' she snaps. And just when it looks like the monotony is going to be broken by a little lively conversation, the door opens again and the receptionist appears: 'Mr Friedmann, please!' I feel like answering: 'Sorry! I haven't got time just now,' but think better of it. They probably already think I'm a weirdo.

I take my leave of the other customers with the words, 'Enjoy your wait.' But one look at the grave, silent faces of my companions-in-waiting tells me that they can't see the funny side of this.

'Well, how are you feeling today?' my doctor greets me with his usual words. 'Impatient,' I reply.

Amazingly good!

At a doctor's surgery in Florida, they have found a way to make waiting a little more exciting. Any patient who has to wait longer than 15 minutes wins a lottery ticket worth $5 and with which they have the chance to win a million dollars. This creates a lighter mood in the waiting room and gives rise to lively conversation. It is also an incentive to the surgery to work as efficiently as possible, as otherwise it will cost them too much.

I need help!

Hospitals are almost my second home. My parents used to think I was just a particularly lively child and that I would calm down as I grew older. Nowadays, they just shake their heads when I tell them of my various little mishaps. I really haven't changed that much. As a kid, I would take a tumble while roller-skating or injure myself playing ice hockey. Nowadays, I damage my knee snowboarding, cut my head playing beach volleyball or dislocate vertebrae in my neck on the golf course. A & E departments haven't changed much since my childhood days either, though in some cases the walls have been painted and even have pictures hung on them. But the procedure for dealing with incoming patients hasn't changed one jot. We might as well still be living in the Stone Age.

Instead of asking me how I feel or whether I am in fact still capable of dealing with the necessary formalities, the man on the reception desk shoves a two-page form at me from behind his glass screen. I have to fill this out before anything can be done to help me. 'Regulations, sir,' he tells me stiffly, seeing me rummaging in my pockets and handing me a pen. Grimacing in pain, I fill in all my personal details and wonder when I am going to get *some* help here. But I wait, and wait, and wait....

After the bad news from the doctor – multiple fractures of

the upper arm – I take up residence in my 'new home'. A room for two with a view of another concrete block and in the bed next to me, a roughly 80-year-old fellow-sufferer. 'They're going to operate tomorrow morning. The anaesthetist will be around to see you,' the nurse tells me, handing me a gown. There's no room for prudery here. I exchange my ski overalls for this little shirt in green and white, which literally leaves nothing to the imagination. The angel in white – my nurse – has to help me because of my injured arm. Then she leaves me to my fate and Mr Hausmann, my roommate.

And it's now, as I lie down on the fully electronic bed and look around me, that I start to feel really, desperately ill. A full-blown case of the hospital blues, I think, noticing the metal arm suspended over my bed, which has various buttons and a device to help me pull myself to a sitting position. I start trying out the various mechanical functions of the bed and entertain myself by pressing a button and watching the head end of the bed slowly rise. If I raised the head end and the foot end at the same time, I think to myself, I could turn myself into a human sandwich.

Next, I examine the console hanging threateningly over my head. It has two illuminated buttons on it with pictograms on them and another button with a pictogram of a female nurse in uniform. One press of this button and the corresponding person will come running... and as I am, after all, in pain, I stretch out my finger and press the belly of the 'nurse' on the button. The pictogram lights up, showing that my call for help is being dealt with.

A few moments later, 'Peter/male nurse' enters the room, taking me completely by surprise. He looks nothing like the nurse on the button. 'Night sister' Peter brings me a painkiller in a little plastic cup that reminds me of the ones they hand out for urine samples at my GP's surgery. He also gives me a sleeping pill – to help me get some rest before my operation next day. I am expected to wash this down with a sip of luke-warm camomile tea from a thermos flask. It makes me gag so hard I nearly spray the walls with it. My last thought as I drift off to sleep is of the guardian angel I am sure has been watching over me since my birth. Despite my various accidents, I have never come to serious harm.

At 5.30 am (!) the door is flung open and some sadistic person turns on the harsh neon lighting. For a moment, I am disoriented. Am I still on earth or have I died and gone to heaven? From the next bed, Mr Hausmann says, 'It's like this every morning.' What a comforting thought. I am not allowed any breakfast or any lukewarm camomile tea – life is tough – so all I can do is lie there like a lamb waiting to be led off to the slaughter. This time, it really is a female nurse who comes to help me out of my 'prison dress' and into an equally trendy plain green gown. Together with another nurse, she pushes my bed and me to the operating suite in the hospital basement. And now I really do feel like the *victim*, lying on my back on my bed, staring at the ceiling lights as they flash past me. I feel really sick – not because I'm afraid of the operation, but from travelling in this unaccustomed position.

A different angel (this time in green) shakes my hand and connects me up to various devices and IVs. Funny-looking angel, I think, in a surgical mask and rubber gloves, as he bombards me with medical jargon. Meanwhile, the surgeons are laying their instruments out and chatting, again in a language I don't understand. I count one, two... and wonder whether I'll ever wake up again. And if I don't, the last thing I see on this earth will be an anaesthetist with greying hair wearing a surgical mask and horn-rimmed glasses.

Amazingly good!

In a clinic in Zurich, you can walk to the operating theatre instead of being pushed there on your bed. When you arrive, you are welcomed and the procedure is explained to you before they administer the anaesthetic.

Another clinic has very successfully managed to lend its rooms a little hotel flair. They are decorated in warm colours, and the towels are soft, brightly coloured and fragrant smelling. The hospital even employs a 'Guest Relation Manager', who visits every patient twice a day, makes a note of what they would like to eat, their preferred reading matter, etc. With her pleasant and cheerful manner, she creates an extraordinarily positive atmosphere.

Language lessons at the florist's

I take a look at my desk planner and see that between *Marketing plan update, 10.00–11.15 am* and *2.00–4.00 pm Regional sales meeting,* I have written, *Visit Grandma!*

My grandmother has lived in a home for the last 11 years, and every three weeks I make time in my busy schedule to drop by and visit her, a pleasure we both enjoy very much. I always take along a little gift, which I select very carefully and according to the motto: variety is the spice of life! It's mid-April, and everyone is looking forward eagerly to the start of spring, so I decide to pay a visit to a garden centre on my way to the home. A slate in front of the store reads, *Get a Taste of Spring at the Seemüller Garden Centre* – just what I'm looking for! I can't see anything I like among the bouquets of spring flowers on display and decide to be creative and put together my own bouquet for Grandma. A young florist appears at my side and asks if she can help me. 'I'd like a nice bunch of pretty spring flowers for my grandmother,' I answer.

As if someone had pressed a button, she starts to reel off the names of the various cut flowers displayed in vases. 'Anemones combined with *muscari armeniacum* would be nice, or perhaps you would prefer *hypericum* with *ranunculus asiaticus?* The *freesia refracta* is also very pretty – they smell so good – perhaps with *myosotis sylvestris?*'

I can't tell one flower from another. My eyes glaze over, and I am reduced to trying to follow her finger as she continues her recital of the Latin names, pointing first at one vase and then at another. 'These *centaurea* last a very long time,' I hear her say. 'Mmmhh – I think a few *myconos sylvester* would be nice – perhaps with, um, these *Cyrano de Ber...* or whatever they're called,' I say, pointing in my turn at a vase of brightly coloured blooms. 'You mean the *myosotis sylvestris* and the *centaurea cyanus?*' I nod and, just to be on the safe side, ask her how much each flower costs, as she starts pulling them one after another out of their vases. At least I get the price in euros and not in some old defunct Latin currency. When I work out what this bouquet is likely to cost me (and I've only got as far as eight flowers), I can feel my pupils widen in shock.

'Er, I think I'll take a potted plant after all,' I hear myself say. 'That will be 18 euros,' says 'Flora'. 'Shall I wrap it in paper or foil?' I remember that my grandmother was always a conservationist and constantly warning us not to buy plastic carrier bags. 'Paper, please,' I say.

So that's what they call A Taste of Spring at the Seemüller Garden Centre. Well, at least I now know for sure that I've forgotten everything I ever learnt in Latin lessons at school.

Amazingly good!

Say it with flowers! And it's much easier if they have a name.

One garden centre realized this and now gives its potted plants male and female Christian names, printed on pretty labels attached to the plant with raffia. On the back of the label, they print instructions for the care of the plant.

Another florist offers a special service. When a customer buys a plant costing more than 100 euros, they offer to visit the customer at home in two months' time to check how the plant is doing.

It's also possible to place a 'subscription' with a florist to ensure that it's always springtime in your home! Many stores will deliver 'tailor-made' bouquets once a week. Men often like to send their wives flowers in this way.

Cats would buy goldfish flakes

Once a year I visit a pet store, usually shortly before Christmas. I don't go there because I'm planning to give someone a pet as a Christmas present, but because we already have a pet – our tomcat Benjamin. Every Christmas, he gets his favourite present – a plastic pot of fish food!

Pet stores always make me slightly uneasy. The idea of buying and selling living creatures, especially our most loyal companions, is not a pretty one. Under the law, animals are considered much the same as any other goods to be bought and sold at will, but that doesn't make it any better.

In the store window, I see a couple of hamsters standing on their hind legs, peering at me with beady black eyes. A dwarf rabbit presses its pink nose against the glass.

I open the door and am immediately engulfed by a wave of a perfume called 'eau de farmyard'. To get to the section with Benjamin's fish flakes, I have to cross the whole store. On my way, I pass numerous boxes and cages containing some of our little friends.

Suddenly, I come face to face with a half-naked African Grey parrot, hunched up on his perch in a cage. This poor devil looks like an exotic cross between a goose (plucked and ready for the oven) and a parrot, but he isn't. No, he has pulled out his own feathers – as the result of psychological stress, out of loneliness, because he has lost his mate or perhaps simply because he lacks affection?

If I could, I would take all the animals with me, build an ark and offer them a better life without human beings knocking on the glass, staring at them, poking and prodding them around.

With my pot of fish food in my hand, I march to the cash desk. Paradoxically, on the back of the till there is a sticker left over from the 1970s. '*Help the animals*', it says. I flee from the shop and head for the 'Vegi Inn' for a spot of – meat-free – lunch.

Amazingly good!

In a large city, I found a pet store that doesn't stock live animals but shows its customers pictures on their computer or videos. Inside, the store looks like a cosy bistro with a seating area, though of course, it still stocks all the food, toys and equipment you need for your pets. If you want a pet, you choose it via computer and order it by mouse click.

When the boss makes a speech

'Dear colleagues! Time flies. Yet another year has passed, and... blah, blah, blah.'

Just three sentences, but from the lips of Herbert Huber, these three little sentences mean the beginning of a very long speech. 'I would like to say just a few words... blah, blah, blah,' he continues, while we, his 'dear colleagues', sit lined up like battery chickens, staring at the soup going cold in front of us.

'With your help, the company has once again fought for and maintained its position on what is becoming an increasingly tough market.' Fight, I think, and in my mind's eye I see our sales manager struggling valiantly on the battlefield with our remaining customers. But surely you only fight enemies? If Mr Huber is already seeing our customers as 'the enemy', perhaps next year we will be spared the ninth edition of the world's most boring speech.

In fact, Mr Huber is not speaking to his subordinates. He is addressing customers, his in-company customers, so to speak. We know the business better than he does. Unlike him, we still have direct contact with our customers, and we don't fight them but advise them and cater to their needs.

The waitress arrives to offer everyone a second helping of soup, though none of us has had a chance to touch our first helping yet. When she reaches me, I nod, hoping that a ladleful of hot soup will raise the temperature of the now cold first bowl to an acceptable level. 'As I see, soup and bread have been served, which reminds me of a favourite saying of my grandfather's, the founder of the company: hard bread is not hard, *no* bread is hard.'

And just as two-thirds of us are reaching for our spoons, hoping that the time for speeches is over at last and dinner can begin, Mr Huber raises his glass of white wine with the words: 'I wish you all a very Merry Christmas and a pleasant evening. Enjoy your meal!'

Enjoy your meal – that's the cue we've been waiting for. At long last we can turn our attention to our stone-cold soup. Having eaten it, we sit with rumbling stomachs and hope the next course won't be long coming.

A loud 'Ho, ho, ho,' followed by the sound of sleigh bells startles us out of our dreams. Instead of the main course, Father Christmas arrives, looking just like he does in all the picture books and carrying a big jute sack over his shoulder. Herbert Huber's face breaks out in a broad grin as he proudly beckons Father Christmas onto the stage.

In accordance with the rules of etiquette, every female and then every male employee is called to the front of the room to receive his or her Christmas gift. Herbert Huber shakes hands with each and every one of them: 'Merry Christmas, Mr Kunze! Merry Christmas, Ms... er...'. 'Keller,' the woman, a secretary from block B, tells him. She shakes hands with her boss, Herbert Huber, whom she has seen perhaps 20 times over the last year.

Everyone opens his or her present. A red pottery angel with a blue loop to hang it up by. 'To match the pottery Father

Christmas from last year,' is my ironical comment, until I remember that I hung last year's present on my neighbour's front door.

'Well, Friedmann – enjoying yourself, I hope?' inquires Herbert Huber as he pauses behind my chair on his way around the room. I ought to suggest that he attend a seminar on customer-orientation, but think better of it. Instead, I pick up my little pottery angel, wave it in the air, raise my eyebrows in an expression of seasonal jollity and boom 'Ho, ho, ho.'

Amazingly good!

Amaze your audience by making your next speech truly interesting and convincing. Making a lasting impression is enough to amaze them.

(And by the way, my company offers tailor-made coaching on appearing and speaking in public, teaching you how to structure a speech for your particular audience and how to phrase it in a customer-oriented manner.)

Project 'Christmas gifts for our customers'

'Everyone has a use for a bottle of wine,' says Elke Kramer, the marketing manager. 'Or has anyone got a better idea?' she asks, looking inquiringly round at us. It's early November, and the management is holding its monthly meeting in *corpore*. We have reached item 7 on the agenda: 'Christmas gifts for our customers'.

'Everyone has a use for a calendar, too, and with our

company name and logo on it, it has greater advertising impact than a bottle of wine.' Herbert Huber's word is law, because Herbert Huber is the CEO.

'Why not give them *nothing* for a change?' Eight pairs of eyes turn to stare at me incredulously. 'What exactly do you mean by that, Friedmann? No Christmas presents for our customers, indeed!' Huber looks at me reproachfully, as if I had just snatched a lollipop from some kid's hand.

I know Herbert Huber likes arguments to be presented in 'firstly, secondly, thirdly' order, so that's exactly the tack I follow as I explain what I mean: 'Firstly, the business climate is not good at the moment, and I think we could put the money to better use. After all, we're not talking peanuts here. It's a matter of some 25,000 euros.'

'Secondly,' I continue, blithely ignoring the fact that Herbert Huber is obviously itching to shoot that argument down in flames, 'everybody gives their customers a calendar or a bottle of wine at Christmas. By New Year, they will have completely forgotten which company gave them which wine, so there doesn't seem to me to be much point. Besides, our customers have received one of those two items from us every Christmas several times over the last few years.'

Then I draw breath for my final argument: 'And thirdly, isn't it a bit late to be thinking about Christmas presents now? It seems to me that every year, Christmas catches us completely unawares.' I make a rhetorical pause here to let my last words sink in, just as I learnt to do from my presentation trainer, Jörg Neumann. I have always found this technique to be very effective when I want to drive my message home.

'My suggestion is' – I carefully avoid making eye contact with any of my colleagues – 'not to give our customers Christmas gifts at all this year. Instead, I think we should select a random day in spring and surprise them with a gift then. I think that would be much more effective.'

Reactions to my proposal vary widely around the table, from 'Not a bad idea,' to 'Unusual, I'll give it that!' or 'No way!' And once everyone has had a chance to speak their mind in their own unique and inimitable way, we do what we always do in such situations. We look expectantly to Herbert Huber, awaiting his final, irrevocable and incontestable decision, which he always introduces with the following words:

'Well, as we don't seem to be able to reach any consensus here, I say let's...'. He breaks off here, but in his case not for rhetorical effect, but to enable him to shuffle the sheaf of paper in front of him into some semblance of order before he continues. 'Mr Friedmann has got a point there, but on the other hand, I can't imagine not giving our customers a gift at all at Christmas. After all, it's a tradition, and traditions are not there to be broken.' His eyes rest briefly on me, and I feel like a schoolboy who has just been taught a valuable lesson for future life. 'I suggest that we donate 5,000 euros to a children's charity and send our customers a card informing them that we have done so.'

'I don't believe this!' I think to myself. Inside, I'm seething. After the bottle of wine and the calendar, this has got to be the third stupidest idea of all. Not the idea of donating money to a children's charity, of course, but the card. If we are going to donate money, let's do it without making a song and dance about it. By announcing our noble gesture to our customers in this way, we are losing the effect of understatement. Besides, the cards serve no useful purpose for our customers, and it's going to cost us a pretty penny to print and mail them, money that would have been better spent if we had donated it to charity straight away.

'Ms Kramer? At our next meeting, I need three proposals for card design and text, please.'

'Any further questions?' Herbert Huber inquires. As far back as I can remember, no one has ever answered this question with a 'Yes,' mainly because his eyes are always firmly fixed on the pad in front of him when he asks it and because his tone is enough to nip any objections in the bud. And today is no exception.

There were, in fact, questions. They weren't to be found written on Herbert Huber's notepad, though, but on the faces of the management. The meeting ends at 11.45 am, having lasted 45 minutes longer than planned, and I leave the room knowing that item 7 on the agenda is not going to surprise our customers at all.

Amazingly good!

In Zurich, there is a company that specializes in providing corporate clients with gifts for their customers. After in-depth consultation and having familiarized themselves with the client's company and customer groups, its creative team suggests appropriately priced, original and, above all, effective gifts.

A particularly effective gift is the 'I visit my customers' method. Punctually at the beginning of spring each year, the sales manageress of a hotel we regularly used for company events would visit us and present us with two large bouquets of colourful spring flowers to thank us for booking with them. Of course we engaged in small talk on such visits. And of course, we will continue to book with them in future.

The team of another hotel amazed us by turning up in our office on the hottest day of summer 2000 and serving ice cream in our offices.

Fully booked

'AlpenresidenzKärntnerturmMyNameIsSandraHowMayIHelp You?'

I hesitate for a second before replying. I'm not sure whether this torrent of words has come to its end yet or not.

'Joe Friedmann here. Good afternoon! I'd like to book a double room…'. Before I can continue, the voice butts in on the other end of the line: 'One moment, please. I'll connect you.'

'ReservationsDeskMyNameIsPetra…'.

'Joe Friedmann speaking. Good afternoon! I'd like to book a double room.'

'When?' Petra asks curtly. 'From 14 to 17 January.'

After a short interlude in which I am entertained with traditional Austrian folk music, Petra returns with the encouraging words: 'Sorry, we're fully booked.'

My quest to find a double room for a weekend skiing break in Austria seems doomed to failure. Petra is the fifth hotel employee in Austria to have dashed my hopes of finding hotel accommodation.

'Is there nothing you can do?' I inquire, hoping that there might be some way they could help me after all.

'No, sorry. Fully booked.' In the background, I can hear

another phone ringing, and I get the feeling Petra is itching to rush off and answer it. I feel like screaming: 'Help! I'm still here and I still need to find a room.' 'Was there anything else, sir?'

'Can you recommend somewhere else I might try?' I inquire timidly. 'Phew! Everyone's fully booked at the moment… but you could try the Kürfürstenhof.' I can tell from the tone of her voice that I'd better not try her patience by asking her for the number.

After such telephone conversations, I feel the urge to rush off and make an appointment with a therapist. It's as if the money is out there lying on the streets but everyone's too lazy to bend down and pick it up. Why, for heaven's sake, didn't Petra at least ask me for my name and address? After all, we might want to book a room with them some other time. A little customer marketing in the meantime wouldn't go amiss. As a salesman, I find this unbelievable. I, a potential customer, phone them. And instead of informing me what services they can provide, all they can tell me is what they *can't* do for me. I strike that hotel from my memory straight away.

In the end, however, I did manage to find a room, and not two weeks later, my girlfriend and I are sitting in the bar of the Hotel Kürfürstenhof. I order cappuccino. 'We don't serve cappuccino, only café au lait,' the Austrian waiter tells me in a friendly but determined tone. He looks bored, and his eyes are already straying to the next table, where two new guests are just sitting down.

'Um, excuse me,' I reply, genuinely surprised. 'Cappuccino is made of just coffee and milk, too. Foamed milk with cocoa powder on the top.'

'Orders from the boss. I can't do anything about it. I can bring you a coffee with *Schlagobers* on the top.'

'Er, what's *Schlagobers*, please?' I inquire. I'm just a poor Central European and unfamiliar with Tony the waiter's Austrian dialect.

'Whipped cream with cocoa on the top.'

'Great!' I tell him, and after consultation with my girlfriend I order two Austrian cappuccinos.

There's another unexpected discovery when we ask for the bill. 'That will be 10 euros and 80 cents,' Tony tells us. We pay and have had quite enough of surprises for one day.

Amazingly good!

At one hotel chain (American, of course!) customers can state whether they would like their bookings confirmed by e-mail, SMS or fax in future.

In one café, I ordered a café au lait. The waitress asked me, 'How much milk would you like in your cafe au lait, sir?'

'An espresso, please,' I said to a waiter in South Tyrol, and was surprised when he inquired: 'Which brand of espresso would you like?' This excellent café offers a variety of coffees. Later he explained laconically, 'There are many different teas, after all. So as coffee specialists, we offer a variety of coffees.'

In Nuremberg, I ordered a cappuccino and when it arrived, there was a heart sprinkled in the foamed milk on the top. Guaranteed to delight anyone!

When prospective customers phone the reservations desk of a hotel on Lake Achen, the staff always make a note of their name and address and ask whether they have a video recorder. Ten days later, they receive a video in the post with a 10-minute film about the hotel and the surrounding area. The friendly accompanying letter reads: 'Pictures say more than a thousand words. We hope this film will introduce you to our hotel and make you look forward to your forthcoming stay with us.'

A very clever idea, because of course, when you have watched the film, you pass it on to friends, unlike a hotel brochure, which is likely to end up in the recycling bin. The hotel owner later told me that on average, five potential new guests watch a film before it is 'disposed of'.

The man from the insurance company

I come through the door of my apartment after a long and exhausting day at work and have just put down my briefcase when the phone rings.

'My name is Kerner. I'm from AOP Insurance and I would like to ask whether you are satisfied with your present insurance,' says a voice on the other end of the line.

A situation we all know. Someone on the other end of the line who wants to sell you something although you have already got everything you need. Of course I'm insured. My car is insured, the contents of my household are insured, my apartment is insured, and I've even insured my cat. Nowadays, everything is insurable, even death.

And once you've taken out the insurance and put all those sheets of paper covered with small print carefully away in the file labelled 'Insurance', you forget all about it. You're only reminded of its existence when you find the bill for the insurance premium in the mail or when something happens and you actually need to file a claim.

'I don't quite understand,' I say to Mr Kerner. Bad move. Now he gives me the standard 10-minute lecture on the advantages of AOP Insurance, in particular their unbeatable prices etc, etc, etc.

'Hello? Are you still there?' he asks when he finally pauses for breath and realizes that there are no signs of life from my end of the line. 'Good question!' I answer provocatively. 'Look, Mr Kerner. I have 38 years of experience with insurance companies, and I know that it's not the insurance company itself that matters, but the relationship between its customers and their personal insurance agent.'

'Oh? So you're in the insurance business, too?' he asks, moving into 'oh-so-we're-colleagues' mode. 'No. Whatever gave you that idea?' I answer innocently. 'But... you just said you have 38 years of experience with insurance companies!' 'Right! I'm 38 years old, and like every other Central European, I've been insured since the day of my birth.'

My answer has taken him completely by surprise! I glance at my watch. Unbelievable! Mr Kerner has wasted 16 minutes of my precious time and has given me absolutely nothing in return. This makes my tone a shade more direct, more provocative and definitely more aggressive.

'Well, you've told me a lot about how good and inexpensive your company is. Now tell me something about yourself!'

'What do you want to know?' he asks uncertainly. My question probably wasn't covered in the instruction manual for insurance salesmen.

'Well, tell me something about your own personal service, the way you advise your customers. For example, when nothing has happened and they don't need to file a claim. How does your service differ from that offered by your colleagues or by my insurance agent?'

He sidesteps the issue: 'The fact is that what the average customer wants is the best possible insurance cover for the lowest premium.'

'No. The fact is that I am not the *average customer*.' (Who wants to be *average*?) 'And I just happen to be absolutely convinced that I am insured with a fairly conventional company but with the best insurance agent in the world. His name is Harry Gisler, and he's always there for me. I hear from him without fail about every two months. Whenever I have had to claim on my insurance, he has taken care of everything for me, from A to Z. He contacts me whenever he can see a way to reduce my insurance premiums or whenever he finds additional cover I need. He knows me, my girlfriend and my son by name, and he would recognize me anywhere in the world.'

'But Mr Fritzmann…!'

'Friedmann! My name is Friedmann!' I correct him. This call has now gone on for 24 minutes, but I can tell that it's nearing its end.

'Tell you what. I'm going to do two things,' he answers, unperturbed. 'I'm going to send you our brochures in the mail and then we can make an appointment so I can give you a better idea of myself and AOP Insurance.'

'Wrong!' I answer. 'I am going to do two things. First, I'm going to wish you a pleasant evening, and second, I'm going to put the phone down.' And I did.

Amazingly good!

My insurance agent knew that I was planning to fulfil a

childhood dream of mine and buy myself a convertible. He gave me the address of a good and fair car dealer, and not five weeks later, I bought a car there. When I got back to the office on that day, there was a large tube of suntan lotion on my desk with a card bearing the friendly words: 'Don't forget to protect yourself, and Happy Travels!'

I had my mobile phone stolen when I was in South Africa. I phoned my insurance agent and asked what I should do. He asked me a couple of questions, then said: 'You just go ahead and enjoy the rest of your holiday. I'll take care of the phone problem!' And he was as good as his word. When I got home, I found a brand-new mobile on my desk with all the necessary paperwork, all filled in and waiting for my signature. All I had to do was sign and thank him.

In the summer of 1999, a heavy hailstorm damaged hundreds of cars. My insurance company seized this opportunity to motivate their frustrated customers. Each customer received an invitation to bring in his or her car for damage assessment. This meant that the insurance company had to deal with hundreds of customers in the space of just a few days. When I drove my badly pockmarked car into the hangar-like building, I couldn't believe my eyes. My insurance agent was standing at the entrance with a glass of fruit juice in his hand. He welcomed me, invited me to get out and accompany him to the Summer Bar the insurance company had set up especially for its clients. While the experts took a look at my car, we had a very pleasant chat. Less than 20 minutes later, someone came and handed me my car keys. When I got home and opened the boot, I found a box of chocolates there. The insurance company had placed one in every car as a surprise gift.

Craftsmen wanted

My grandfather used to say that if you are a craftsman, you will never be short of work. For him, a craftsman was anyone who worked with their hands – whether joiner, stonemason, painter or electrician. They all have one thing in common: everyone needs them at some time in their lives. I leaf through the *Yellow Pages* in search of an electrician. I need two big lamps put up and three new sets of wiring installed. A simple matter for those who know what they're doing, a nightmare for someone who is all thumbs like me.

All-Round Electrical Services. Fast – competent – reliable! I read below the name of the Leuchter AG. Sounds good, I think to myself, and dial the number. The phone rings five times, and then I hear the call being rerouted. It rings another four times and then someone shouts 'Hello?'

'Is that the Leuchter AG?' I ask uncertainly.

'Yes!' is the curt reply.

'Good morning. My name is Joe Friedmann. I need your help. I need a few...' but I get no further, because he interrupts me: 'No chance this week. We're fully booked.' I can hear the sound of loud drilling in the background.

He makes a note of my name and address and says they will call me back. A week passes, and I'm starting to wonder whether he actually understood me with all that noise going on behind him, when out of the blue, he calls me. It's Saturday lunchtime and I'm doing some shopping when my mobile rings: 'Müller, Leuchter AG. I'm in your neighbourhood at the moment. I could fit you in after lunch.'

I had intended to be at home when the electrician came, but I decide not to change my plans, to carry on with my shopping trip and not to postpone a visit to a friend afterwards. So I ring my girlfriend and tell her that an electrician will be calling after lunch. 'And please don't forget to ask him how much it will cost before he starts!' I remind her, not wanting any unpleasant surprises.

As I park my car in front of the house later that afternoon, a minibus labelled *Leuchter AG. All-Round Electrical Services. Fast – competent – reliable!* is just driving off. Behind the wheel sits a man with a cigarette in his mouth, mobile phone at his ear. Laden with my carrier bags full of shopping, I enter my flat, looking forward to admiring our new lighting. I find my girl-friend in a very bad mood as she pushes the vacuum cleaner around the flat. What she had to say on the subject of crafts-men doesn't bear repeating, so I'll just give you a summary:

- The electrician left dirty footprints all over our carpet and black fingerprints on our white-painted walls.

- Even the new lamps were dirty.

- Our apartment reeked of cigarette smoke, even though he hadn't smoked inside the building.

- His report was illegible, except for the figure at the bottom, which, in contrast, was perfectly clear: 210 euros!

- Beneath every hole he had drilled, there was a little pile of dust left for us to clear away.

Yes, you'll never be short of work if you're a craftsman.

Amazingly good!

One master painter from Graz in Austria guarantees to leave

his customers' homes spotless. If any of his employees leave a mess behind, the customer can have the room cleaned professionally at the company's expense. It goes without saying that they have never had to get professional cleaners in. Their staff always clean up behind themselves. But this guarantee makes a good impression on potential customers even before they decide to hire this company.

A firm installing new kitchens cuts a postcard-sized piece out of the material the customer has chosen for the cabinet fronts and writes on it: 'In exactly three weeks from now, you will be the proud owner of a new kitchen, so go ahead and invite people round for dinner! Thank you for your custom!' And then he sends this 'postcard' to the customer, to great effect!

Another painter always phones his customers a few months after doing a painting job to ask them whether they are happy with the new colour scheme. This often leads to other jobs they need doing. In addition, when he has finished a painting job, he presents the customer with a bottle of paint in the corresponding colour, together with a new paintbrush. Customers can then paint over any scratches that occur in the course of time themselves.

Two customers less

This is the fourth shoe shop I have entered today. I'm looking for elegant men's shoes in brown, and I think I might just be in luck here. I've seen a pair I like in the window.

As I step out of the lift, I see shoes, shoes, and more shoes, but there is no shop assistant in sight to help me. Ok, I think, I'll find the shoes from the shop window myself, and I wander up and down the aisles looking at the shelves. There are 7, 7½,

8... 8 ½ – that's my size. I search the rows of shelves from top to bottom. They're full of shoes, but I can't find the ones I saw in the window. In my mind, I can already hear a shop assistant telling me: 'Sorry, we've sold out of your size.' I hear those words often, and not only when I'm shopping for shoes.

It's a very upmarket shop, but definitely understaffed. I've just decided to look for someone to help me on the floor below when a woman approaches me. She's in her mid-40s and enveloped in a cloud of perfume. 'Can I help you?' she asks, straightening up a pair of size 7s on a shelf.

I tell her I saw *just* what I'm looking for in the window, and I can see she doesn't like what she hears. And here they are, those words I've been dreading: 'If they're not on the shelves, we don't have them.' As I already mentioned, I've heard those words many times before, so I switch to Plan B, a plan that has worked many times before, though it's something a shop assistant should think of without any prompting from me, the customer.

'What about the shoes I saw in the window? Might they be size 8½?' I ask hopefully. 'Just a moment. I'll look and see.' She strolls towards the stairs at a leisurely pace, stopping to chat briefly to a colleague, and disappears into shoe Never-Never-Land, or so it seems. It's a full eight minutes before she returns. But at least she has good news for me. Plan B has done the trick again!

The shoes fit well, but cost more than I had been planning to spend – 180 euros, I think, is a lot of money for a pair of shoes. I try to quell my misgivings by reciting to myself all the arguments in favour of my buying them. Expensive shoes last longer, are more comfortable. They're handmade, have a better shine, and so on. Besides, if I cut back on visits to the cinema and eating out for a while, I can easily afford them.

I follow the shop assistant to the cash desk, where a young lady who has just entered the store beats me to it. She takes a pair of high-heeled ladies shoes out of a plastic bag. 'I would like to exchange these,' she says, pointing to the bent heel of the left shoe. The shoes are a very upmarket brand, so I expect them to give her another pair without further ado. But no: the shop assistant wants the receipt. 'I can't give you another pair if you don't have the receipt,' she says in an unfriendly tone.

'But they cost 150 euros, and you stock this label. It says so in your window. I bought these shoes on holiday in Ticino. You can't expect me to drive 600 kilometres just to exchange a pair of shoes!'

'Sorry. There's nothing I can do about it,' the shop assistant answers firmly, shrugging her shoulders, as if her words alone hadn't been enough to express her total lack of concern.

The young lady leaves the shop, close to tears, and the battleaxe shop assistant passes my shoes over the scanner. 'Stop!' I say. 'On second thoughts, I don't think I will buy them after all. From what I've just seen, I get the feeling it's not a good idea to spend so much money in this store.'

'As you wish,' she answers, totally unimpressed. 'I'll cancel the sum, then.'

'You do that,' I answer. 'And be sure to tell your marketing department you've just lost two customers.'

Amazingly good!

Some years ago, the manufacturers of a well-known brand of leisure footwear advertised one of their models using the slogan: 'The only thing that will ever need replacing is the laces.' I bought a pair of these shoes in the United States and wore them regularly, at least twice a week.

After three and a half years, the back part of the sole came loose, and I was about to throw them away when I remembered their advertising slogan. I packed the shoes up and sent them to the company headquarters in Germany. I had no receipt, so I just sent a brief accompanying letter. Two weeks later, I received a parcel containing a brand new pair of my favourite shoes together with a letter from the company apologizing for the inconvenience and explaining that the problem had been caused by a production fault affecting a small proportion of the shoes. Wow! You will not be surprised to hear that I have been buying their shoes for the last 18 years.

3 You need cheese to catch a mouse

Pay effective compliments

A compliment is like a sandwich: something special between two slices of the ordinary.

Marlene Dietrich

The dictionary says:

Compliment (Fr.) (flattery).
Praise (mark of appreciation, esteem).

Personally, I prefer to speak of compliments rather than of praise. The reason is the effect on the recipient. Even though the two are very similar, I am convinced that a compliment touches the heart of the recipient more than praise. For me, praise has more to do with logic and rational thinking. It seems to me that it is much harder to pay people a compliment than to praise them. That is my subjective impression.

What do you think is more difficult: making a complaint or paying a sincere compliment?

It's a tough question to answer. Some people find it difficult to criticize the quality of a product. They would rather accept a fault (albeit unwillingly) than complain about it openly to the person who is selling the product to them. Others find it impossible to praise a sales assistant directly and sincerely when he or she has served them well. Human beings are a very complex and baffling species.

Yet there are many different ways of paying someone a compliment. Then why don't we do it more often? Because we lack the courage! We go home and tell our friends and families what outstanding service we got instead of telling the sales assistant face to face. Yet a compliment from us, the customers, is the sales assistant's motivation! He or she needs to know they are doing their job well. They might not have a boss who knows how to motivate them, who knows how to provide honest and open feedback on their job performance. In that case, they will be all the more dependent on a compliment from you!

The beginners' guide to paying compliments

A very effective and impressive exercise!

We know that when we send someone an invoice, it often won't be paid on time. That means we have to write reminders, make phone calls, etc. In the end, we spend a lot of time and money getting what is owed to us. I have never understood why we expend such a lot of energy on those who fail to pay punctually instead of rewarding those who settle their bills on time.

So, in our company, an employee contacts all those customers who pay their bills promptly. This employee will either call them or send them a card, for example with the following text: 'Dear Alexandra Furrer, Thank you very much for settling the invoice with our consultancy fee so promptly. This gave us great pleasure and will motivate us to provide you with service of the same high standard in future!'

Try it out for yourself and you will be amazed at the reactions you get!

I have become a much happier person since I decided to have the courage of my convictions, especially when it comes to praising people for outstanding performance. Just look into someone's eyes as you pay them a compliment and you will see what I mean! I would like to give you two examples that illustrate what amazing results a compliment can have. And then I will offer four tips on how to pay effective compliments.

A 'Mexican wave' in the kitchen

Anyone who has read my book *1001 Tips zur Mitarbeitermotivation* (*1001 Tips on Motivating Your Staff*) will know that I frequently conduct motivation seminars. During just such a seminar, I was sitting at lunch with 12 executives from the automobile industry. The lunchtime buffet in the hotel we were at had been prepared with such love and creativity that everyone went back for seconds – and thirds – and was full of praise. 'Fantastic', 'Bombastic', 'Wow!', 'I've never seen anything like it!' were just some of the comments I heard from my seminar group. Everyone was absolutely delighted with the delicious lunch they had prepared for us. Then the waitress came to our table and asked, 'Was everything to your satisfaction?' I couldn't believe my ears when I heard the lukewarm comments from around our table! 'Yes, very nice,' or a mere, 'Yes, thank you,' was all they said.

When the waitress had left, I decided to tackle them about this: 'Hey, what's wrong with you lot? You call yourselves motivators?' After a short discussion, they agreed that they should have been more direct, more open and above all more enthusiastic in their praise. That was the end of that, you might think, but I suggested we should all march into the kitchen, line up in a row in front of the chefs and give them a 'Mexican wave' like they do in big football stadiums. 'No, we couldn't. March into the kitchen? They'll think we're crazy!' But I refused to let them off the hook, so up we got, and instead of heading for the exit, we marched straight into the kitchen, lined up in a row in front of half a dozen chefs who all eyed us suspiciously. We bowed deeply, one after another, with raised arms and with a loud 'Ooooooohhhh'.

For a second, there was absolute silence. Then the head chef, looking dumbfounded, asked gravely: 'Was something not in order?'

'On the contrary!' we replied. 'That was the best seminar lunch we ever had, and we wanted to tell you ourselves and face to face.' Broad grins appeared on the faces of all the chefs.

At 3.30 pm, we took a coffee break. The hotel manager came up to us and told us that his chefs were still talking about our little 'performance'. They were delighted and said that it was the best compliment anyone had ever paid them.

With one courageous little gesture, we had given those chefs a pleasant surprise that they would be talking about for a long time to come!

Shopping is stressful

It was just a few days before Christmas, and I was fighting my way through a gigantic shopping mall like hundreds of other consumers in the pre-Christmas frenzy. I knew exactly what I wanted, but I didn't know where to find it. The crush was worst at rush hour in the food department. Screaming kids, stressed-out parents, busy managers elbowing others out of the way, tourists with time on their hands – the world and his dog were there.

Five things stood between me and freedom:

1. mustard with green pepper;

2. a bottle of olive oil, extra virgin;

3. lemon grass;

4. pistachio ice cream;

5. 200 grams of Parmesan.

I was standing in front of the shelves with the preserves, looking in vain for mustard with green pepper. If we had been playing that old children's game, and if someone had been looking down on me from the bird's eye perspective, they would have shouted: 'Cold, you're stone cold!' But help was at hand. A female shop assistant came my way, and as our eyes met, I said: 'I'm looking for mustard, the special sort with green pepper...'. 'Yes, we do sell that, but you're three aisles off course!' she said. Somehow she must have seen that I am not exactly an experienced shopper. She asked: 'What else do you need?' I showed her my list. She studied it briefly and said: 'Ok, then! Off we go!' I followed her, and less than five minutes later we were standing at the checkout, me clutching my basket with all the items on my list.

What an incredibly friendly gesture, I thought, especially when you think how stressful the weeks before Christmas are for staff in the retail trade. I had had enough after only 10 minutes in the packed store, and she had probably been on her feet for hours. Just as she was turning away to help the next customer, I said: 'If there was an Oscar for friend-liness and helpfulness, it would go to you.' 'Oh... thank you! We don't very often hear things like that,' she replied bashfully.

I was really glad my courage hadn't deserted me. The smile on her face was like getting an early Christmas present.

Four tips on how to pay successful compliments

1. Never compliment someone for an average service!

2. Always look people in the eye when you are paying them a compliment.

3. Pay your compliment immediately. Don't wait for the 'right' moment.

4. Always express your compliment in your own words and spon-taneously. Anything else will seem false, rehearsed and will have a negative effect.

Complain, but do it properly!

Expectantly, you cut into your expensive steak, but with the very first bite, you realize that what you have on your plate doesn't taste like the 'tender beefsteak from local herds' advertised on the menu, but more like something carved from a cow on its last legs.

'Was everything to your satisfaction?' the waiter asks as he takes away your plate. Statistics show that in this situation, 70 per cent of us will mutter an embarrassed 'Yes,' meekly pay the bill and leave the restaurant. Statistics also show that on average, we will tell at least 10 other people about this negative experience.

Whether you are in a restaurant, in a boutique, at the hairdresser's or at your garage: don't simply accept faults, complain! The advantage for you is that you get the faulty goods replaced, and for the providers of the service or the manufacturers that they can remedy the fault and will gain satisfied customers as a result. But that won't happen if you only complain behind their backs, so to speak. It is dishonest and wrong to accept the faults others make, and no one benefits in the end. In my opinion, the important factor is how you make your complaint.

Six tips on how to complain effectively

1. Before voicing a complaint, assure yourself that the fault is not the result of deliberate action or even malicious intent.

2. Always address your complaint to one person and address them by name. In this way, you are establishing a relationship with this person. In most cases, they will then feel a moral obligation to help you.

3. Complain immediately; in other words, after the first bite of steak and not when you have finished your meal. Complain on the spot wherever possible. Don't wait until you get home and then write a letter. Letters are easy to ignore.

4. Voice your complaint in a very friendly, pleasant tone. People are more likely to be sympathetic to your cause if you are polite. In our heart of hearts, we all like to help others, and your appeal has a better chance of success if the sales assistant can see things from your point of view. Shouting and throwing your weight around turns people against you and will weaken your chances of success.

5. Stick to the facts and don't exaggerate ('I had to wait half an hour for someone to take my order!'). Ignore this advice, and you only give them ammunition to use against you.

6. Don't forget to thank them for taking care of your complaint and for their readiness to help you!

What happened to generosity?

It's unbelievable how petty some sales staff can be when it comes to dealing with complaints.

An impressive example of this is when you order a bottle of wine and discover when you taste it that it is 'corked'. I have seen cases where guests complained about corked wine and in the end, there were three waiters standing around the table trying to persuade them that they were mistaken – and all over a bottle of wine that costs 35 euros in the restaurant (purchasing price for the restaurant, 10 euros). Of course, other guests soon became aware of what was going on, and it was obviously embarrassing for the guest making the complaint, but instead of just accepting the complaint graciously and discreetly bringing a fresh bottle, the waiters apparently decided that attack was the best means of defence.

In the end, it's not worth the argument. The owners of the restaurant can get any bottle replaced free of charge by the wine supplier. All they have to do is save the bottle and attach a label reading 'Corked'.

I have conducted many training courses for waiters in my life, but it never ceases to amaze me how prejudiced they are against their guests. 'They do it on purpose!', 'It's not corked at all!', 'Anybody could say that!', 'They're just taking advantage, showing off!' are some of the comments I hear.

An outraged hotelier once suggested that our company should hold a training course for the hotel, but for the guests, not the staff. Needless to say, he no longer runs a hotel.

It is amazing how negative some people's attitude is – and that in a field where it is their job to make their guests feel welcome. Often, as I have already shown, the opposite is the case. Instead of giving to the guests, they take from them.

Of course there are guests who will brazenly take advantage in certain situations. But they hardly ever make up more than 2 per cent of all guests. So I ask you: why should the other 98 per cent suffer for these 2 per cent? In my opinion, it is much more important that customers know that if there is something wrong with the goods or the service they are paying for, something will be done about it.

Many years ago, a US shoe manufacturer realized how important it was to give customers this sense of security. In their advertisements, this company stated that if they were dissatisfied with the product in any way or if there were any defects, they would receive a pair of new shoes of the same quality immediately.

Their competitors rubbed their hands in glee when they heard this, convinced that this was going to be a huge marketing flop. Far from it! After one year, the shoe company offering this guarantee saw that only 2.9 per cent of their customers took unfair advantage of their offer and demanded a new pair of shoes for no valid reason. The other 97 per cent of their customers were so reassured by this offer that their brand experienced an image boost. Of course, the marketing experts in the company had already thought about this before launching the campaign and had calculated their selling prices to cover losses of 3.5 per cent.

4 And the winner is...

Win the 'Joe Friedmann Customer Amazement Award'!

Over the last few years, I have been able to convince many people of the effectiveness of my customer amazement strategy. Many managers have introduced it in their companies, much to the benefit of their customers.

This gave me the idea for the 'Joe Friedmann Customer Amazement Award', which was presented for the first time in summer 2004. The award goes to the person who has amazed his or her customers most.

How it works

On our website, at www.nzp.ch, you can describe how you, as a customer, have been most amazed and nominate the person

who amazed you with outstanding service. You are not allowed
to nominate yourself!

The winner is selected by a jury of six (three women and
three men) and is made up of customers, representatives of
companies supplying goods and services, and me.

Both the person with the best customer amazement strategy
and the person who nominates them win a prize.

The following are some of the criteria on the basis of which
the jury make their decision:

- how amazed the customer was;
- originality;
- customer-orientation;
- the lasting effect of the strategy;
- practical relevance;
- the advertising impact;
- cost–value ratio;
- uniqueness.

Closing date

The closing date is 31 May of each year. Nominations can be
made up to and including this date.

The 'Joe Friedmann Customer Amazement Award'
was presented for the first time on 18 September 2004 in
Lucerne.

Procedure

Nominations can only be made using the special form provided on our home page at www.nzp.ch.

The winner and their nominator will be notified by post and invited to attend the presentation ceremony in Lucerne.

The prizes

The winner receives the 'Joe Friedmann Customer Amazement Award' in the form of a challenge cup and an amazing weekend in Switzerland.

The person who nominated them receives an amazing weekend for two in Lucerne.

Confidentiality

All information supplied will be treated as strictly confidential. Names will only be published with the consent of those concerned.

Cost

Entry is free of charge.

Questions?

For further information on the 'Joe Friedmann Customer Amazement Award', contact: Daniel Zanetti, NeumannZanetti & Partner, Huobmattstrasse 5, CH-6045 Meggen, Switzerland. Tel: 0041 41 3797777, e-mail: daniel@nzp.ch, website: www.nzp.ch.

The judges' decision is final and no legal recourse is possible.

NeumannZanetti & Partner reserve the right to make alterations to any of the information given here without prior notice. Please refer to our home page at www.nzp.ch for the latest details concerning this award.

The customer has the last laugh

As a customer, you are the judge. This puts you in a position of power. You should not, however, abuse this power. Be a fair and impartial judge.

You had to wait a long time for your spaghetti in a restaurant? Be generous; give the restaurant team another chance. With hindsight, you will often see that the one time you had a long wait was an exception. Mistakes happen. And not only in restaurants.

Whereas I advocate giving people a second chance in the case of delays or quality defects, I demand the maximum penalty when it comes to unfriendliness. And the maximum penalty is not reporting them, but to ignore them. Take your custom elsewhere and tell as many people as possible *what* happened, *where* and *how*. That way, other people won't go there either and you will hit them in the wallet, where it hurts most.

No matter how unfriendly or unprofessional the treatment you receive, you will always be the winner in the end, because you are the customer!

Index